Words and the Word

The Use of Literature as a Practical Aid to Preaching

Canon Bill Anderson

GRACEWING

First published in 2010

Gracewing
2 Southern Avenue
Leominster
Herefordshire HR6 0QF

ISBN 978 0 85244 745 1

Typeset by Action Publishing Technology Ltd
Gloucester GL1 5SR

In memory of my parents

Words and the Word

Contents

Preface

This book brims, beyond its many well-chosen quotations, with the wise and gentle words of a wise and gentle man, and a fine preacher too. How good – to pick up a phrase from its *Introduction* – that this aged Roman Catholic priest has ventured to distil in these precious pages his homiletic experience. May they be both read and heeded!

The exhilarating scope of its title – *Words and the Word* – may seem almost undercut by its sober subtitle: *The Use of Literature as a Practical Aid to Preaching*. But the value of Fr Anderson's book lies in its very bi-polarity. On the one hand, here are practical ways of enhancing the word delivered from the 'mountain' of the pulpit (usually not so lofty these days); on the other, here are some of the great themes that pervade theology and life. This duality seems utterly right. And both aspects are illumined, not obscured, by reference to the preacher's own biography. So, this *is* a book that seminarians, deacons, priests, even bishops, would do well to take in hand. Indeed, conveyed with suitable tact, what a wonderful present for priest friends! But it would be a loss were it confined to the clergy. Just as a good sermon will lead its listeners beyond appreciation of a preacher's learning or eloquence to simple apprehension of the 'thing' itself, the *res* of the celebrated mystery, the presence of the Lord, and its consequences for our lives, so this book both opens a door into our literary inheritance and edges us again and again towards the universal questions: What is literature? What is the relationship of the great literary works of humanity – the 'secular scriptures' – to the Word and words of Christianity and its Jewish antecedent? How might we enter into this literary world, and integrate our human culture with our Christian faith? How might a *lectio humana* enrich our *lectio divina*, and vice versa? How might I finally educate myself?

When St Paul preached to the men of Athens in the middle of the Areopagus, he quoted Greek poets. In a patristic dictum beloved of St Thomas Aquinas, 'Everything true, by whomsoever said, comes from the Holy Spirit' – and, we may add, if it is well said, so much the better. So, as Hugo Rahner said in his great book *Greek Myths and Christian Mystery*, Homer is holy for us Christians too. 'Guided by the genius of poetry, this blind singer touched with trembling hands the primal forms of truth, and for us this makes him the forerunner of the Word that appeared to us clothed in the flesh of man.' Surely every word that is true, beautiful and good can be found again, and should be, in the service of the Word made flesh, and add its lustre to the halting words of preachers.

Fr Anderson has done a service to us all by living in this noble tradition, by preaching from it for half a century, and now leaving us this limpid exposition of it.

Abbot Hugh Gilbert, OSB

Introduction

I begin this reflection with a brief 'apologia', attempting to justify an aged Roman Catholic priest's venturing to publish the fruits of many years of preaching to a variety of congregations.

Words, poetry and drama in particular, have always interested me. Home, school and university served to further my zeal, and I am grateful for having had a classical training in Edinburgh and Cambridge. Theological schooling in Rome was less thrilling, but one aspect of it, preaching, appealed to me more and more. Indeed it is possible that, through the dual thrust of my education (theological and classical), I was led to explore the idea of a linkage between these two areas of 'writtenness' named throughout as 'sacred' and 'secular' scriptures respectively.

My opening chapter relies on the insights of two eminent scholars, focusing on what I myself have felt for a long time: that there is a relationship between the Word of God and words (or language) in general. Fr Timothy Radcliffe, OP, former Master General of the Dominican Order, and Professor Nicholas Boyle, Fellow of Magdalene College, Cambridge, have made me appreciate this better. Radcliffe examines the correlation of the development of words and their preparatory place in awaiting the advent of God's Word in an almost cosmic approach to literature. 'Our story,' he avers, 'begins with God speaking a word, and Creation comes to be.' He savours humanity's search for words allowing us, through taking pleasure in the particular, to reach out to the universal. Pushing this line of thought further, Boyle maintains that a book becomes literature by using language for what he engagingly calls 'the purposeless purpose of enjoyment'.

By showing that life matters – hence sharing in the work of the Spirit – literature lets us delight in this truth about human existence, the truth that 'its constitution is inescapably moral'. Literature, then, is seen to sustain the momentum of God's word. Indeed the hub of Boyle's thinking, and a continuing stimulus to my own work, is contained in his sentence: 'That is the glory of poetry, and of secular literature generally, that out of such slight material as the pleasure to be had from the weaving together of words, it can make analogues of revelation that can illuminate and affect the whole of our life.'

'Analogues of revelation': a claim at one with a cosmic approach to literature, and one which richly suggests a vital connection between the place of Holy Writ and the place of secular writtenness in the spiritual advancement of humanity. My first chapter looks at the consequences of such a claim in both comedy and tragedy in real life and in literature, and calls upon Aristotle and his thoughts about *mimesis* to buttress the notion that such 'representation', the imitation of things, is (Boyle's words) 'the secular analogue of Redemption'.

The essence of the matter, from a Catholic viewpoint, must be that if the Church's convictions about human life are true, we should expect literature which accurately mirrors life to reflect them, whether the authors are Catholic or not.

The remaining key reflection of this chapter, brief but crucial, comes from these words of Seamus Heaney: 'We go to poetry, we go to literature in general, to be forwarded within ourselves. The best it can do is to give us an experience that is like foreknowledge of certain things which we already seem to be remembering.'[1] Perhaps that postulates some kind of 'religious sense' deep within us all. It certainly supports the assertion of Professor Boyle that 'literature is language free from instrumental purpose, and it seeks to tell the truth', and is in tune with the idea that secular literature may serve as the 'prolegomena' to the Bible.

For the preacher, the opening chapter evidently contains much room for encouragement, and exciting possibilities for priests with a love of letters. I dare to hope that an end result of this study is that for those in training for the priesthood there may be a sharpening of the homiletic appetite among any who care to read it. I hope also that any lay readership may find something of interest and enjoyment, even, perhaps, of recognition.

Chapter Two unavoidably introduces some auto-biography, not for its own sake, but to show how this writer's acquaintance with words and with the use of words was sharpened and broadened in two very different ways: first with BBC Scotland's Religious Department for eight years, and second at the Pontifical Scots College in Rome, where the bishops invited me to be the students' Spiritual Director. Thus I had succeeding opportunities to apply my energies to broadcasting and to individual, confidential contact with students. Privileged and happy in both posts, I can only hope that constant involvement with speech and communication helped me to teach and preach better myself, and perhaps to aid others of all ages to improve their skills too. As will be seen in the chapter itself, an offshoot of my Roman duties was to oversee the students' preparation and training in the art of preaching (homiletics) – at once a pleasurable and inhibiting challenge! It will be seen how and to what extent I was able to attract the seminarians towards a literary interest, and what kind of material, poetry especially, was employed in this regard. The mixture of mutual gifts was agreeably piquant, some of the senior men being better versed in theology than I was, and I seeming to have the literary edge over them! The important thing was that we all wanted to learn, in the spirit of the Latin term *discipulus*, which carries not only the meaning of 'learner' but of one *willing* to learn.

I have entitled the third chapter 'Stimuli' by way of making it clear whence my passion for literature arose, and how certain passages of literature have alerted my interest and made me move forward to a wider enthusiasm. As a priest and a preacher, the beauty and power of so much fine writing has entered my ministerial bloodstream. The selection of stimuli reflects stages in my life and is inevitably heterogeneous: from Keats, Shaw, Thompson, Dickens, Hopkins and Duff Cooper. They all seem strongly to come within Professor Boyle's succinct assertion that 'literature is language free from instrumental purpose, and it seeks to tell the truth'. Their range is considerable too – romantic, spiritual, comical, reflective, all are there, singly or amalgamated. I conclude the chapter with germane quotations from Nicholas Boyle and Fr Daniel O'Leary respectively, and have tried to slay that old, insidious enemy of the litterateur – self-indulgence.

Chapter Four leads into a consideration of preaching as 'praxis', and reviews something of the ecclesial background to preaching, whilst acknowledging that much contemporary Catholic preaching in our own land and time is often inadequate. Some modern opinions are reinforced by a deliciously mischievous passage from Chaucer's unprincipled Pardoner!

The role of preaching within the liturgy, and the homily's need to provide spiritual nourishment are then considered. As for the preacher himself, his task of proclaiming the Gospel should be seen not as a liturgical chore, but as an exciting pastoral opportunity. The more it is seen as working for the Lord within a missionary Church, the more fruitful and fulfilling the challenge.

The priest's role as a preaching 'instrument' is illustrated from lines of John Donne, and my reflection presses the musical analogy a little further.

The homily's history is again referred to with the help of advice from St Augustine and St Ephraim, before I move on to the literary beauty of the Bible itself and to what is meant by the expression 'secular scripture'. There is a harking-back to the Boylian claims and definitions, and a compelling extract from an essay by Fr Daniel Francis (within a volume called *Theology and Preaching*), the centrepiece of which reads: 'The pulpit is a mountain. The preaching moment supplies the necessary experience of liminality, the "between space" or threshold for the encounter with God.'[2] I would opine that a constituent of effective liminality could be the use of literature as the 'prolegomena' of biblical proclamation.

After briefly examining the import of Pope John Paul II's Apostolic Exhortation, *Pastores Dabo Vobis*, the chapter ends with contrasting excerpts from poems by R. S. Thomas and Fr Paul Murray, OP, respectively.

I have given the fifth chapter the title 'A Literary Learning Curve'. Having of necessity reverted briefly to a reminder of 'where I am coming from' in this work, I address the matter of the preparatory requirements for preaching an effective homily. A lovely passage of St Athanasius states clearly that left to themselves preachers would be helpless, but that relying on God all will be well, since 'everything according to its own nature is given life and subsistence by him; and through him a wonderful and divine harmony is produced'.

Some stress is laid upon the value of the preacher's building up over time a private treasure-trove, remembered or written down, of lines of all sorts culled from literary sources for possible inclusion in homilies. In this pursuit I continue to hold that 'sacred' and 'secular' scripture are each concerned with truth, the expression of it in the Bible, the quest for it outside the Bible.

The need for flexibility in a preacher's approach in general, and in the use of literature in particular, prompts some reference to Fr Robert Hendrie's recent book, *Go, Tell Them*.[3] This leads on to instances of just such flexibility known to myself from my broadcasting days and from the Rev. Sydney Smith. The learning curve cannot but be protracted.

It is argued that a deeper involvement in public worship will accrue to all, the more literature and the Arts as a whole are available to them. A particularly telling quotation is offered from the US Bishops' publication of 1982, *Fulfilled in Your Hearing*.

Reviewing areas of writing which may serve to stimulate priests' acquaintance with worthwhile and relevant literature, I go on to consider hymns, of which Dr Ian Bradley holds that they provide 'a more familiar and accessible source of teaching about the Christian faith than the Bible'. The question is then addressed: how many hymns can be classed as literature? In Part II of this exposition I attempt to show how a complete homily may be based upon the words and ideas of a fine hymn, in this case *Lead, kindly light.*

Out of the vast prose treasury to hand, this writer pursues 'Autolycus-like investigations' by instancing three favourite anthologies, and by nodding appreciation in passing towards Caryll Houselander and Henri Nouwen.

Drama is inevitably referred to also, though a closer assessment of Shakespeare's dominance is reserved for the chapter following. Poetry, however, other than the Bard's, is discussed at some length, partly perhaps since it is closest to my own heart, but mainly because its intensity and succinctness lend themselves best to incorporation within the limits of the typical Catholic homily of seven to ten minutes' duration.

Certain poems universally recognized as 'great' are mentioned, though a goodly representation of more modern authors occurs. Among them a place had to be found for poets from the Great War, whose reflections are as penetrating for our generation as they were for that of our grandparents. Gerard Manley Hopkins and R. S. Thomas keep breaking in too, both of them veering regularly towards moroseness. Yet the point is made that, when we find 'pleasure' (so crucial for Professor Boyle) in the sadder experiences of humanity, it derives from the consolation that is the *sharing* of grief.

Scottish poetry is not neglected, not only for the obvious reason that I am a Scot preaching mostly to fellow-Scots, but because the best of the poets – Muir, McCaig, Mackay Brown, say – are culturally well-placed to communicate with their ain folk, church-walls notwithstanding. Of the Americans it will be seen that Emily Dickinson has pride of place. The brevity of nearly all her work, and the brevity *within* that brevity enshrining the richest reflections, make her a wonderful source for the homilist looking especially for an arresting opening or an apt conclusion.

Humour in preaching is nervously mentioned rather than favoured, and the chapter concludes with three 'slants' upon preaching from disparate sources, including one derived from Yves Congar. As the old scholastics averred: *Quidquid recipitur, ad modum recipientis accipitur.* ('Whatever is received is received after the manner of the receiver'.)

Shakespeare is the protagonist in Chapter Six, with special reference to *The Tempest*, and to recent productions in Stratford-on-Avon. Thereafter matters of style are assessed, and there is a concluding section on the importance of the preacher's holiness. That Boyle should have elected to focus on *The Tempest* helps us better to grasp his theories about literature and make a practical examination of them. Pursuing his stance on the 'revelatory role' of literature, he holds that 'fiction' in the widest sense 'puts into words or into mimic show things that, before we heard and saw them, we did not know we knew'. That statement, already adumbrated within this argument in a quotation from Seamus Heaney, is quite crucial for the development of my position. Concentrating particularly on the moment when Miranda cries: 'O brave new world /That has such people in't!', and Prospero replies, ''Tis new to thee', Boyle demonstrates how, in those few words, the whole 'world' – as the characters call it – is seen 'in a light at once multiple and strangely clear, like a landscape after the storm that gives the play its title'. So forceful is Boyle's insight that another brief example must be given: 'But there is another world still that the words of Miranda and Prospero let us glimpse, behind even the world of the text, another world about which the play is telling us – or allowing us to sense – the truth.' This section of his approach is as thrilling as it is convincing, and encapsulates what I have felt with passion over many years, without the ability to formulate it exactly.

Reeling a little under the brilliance of the Boylian synthesis, I then turn my attention to some of the performers and performances of Shakespeare seen by me over time, and especially within the 2006–2007 season at Stratford-on-Avon. I have tried to show how the 'revelatory' aspect shines through continually in the plays, and how the 'extinction of personality', commended in the finest authors by Boyle, T. S. Eliot and others, is perfected by Shakespeare, 'out-topping knowledge'.

There follow some short musings upon style, as I move temporarily away from the central thrust. Nevertheless, the practical ministry of preaching, however solid, however true its substance, will fare ill if it is defective in communicative skill. Authorities on the matter are cited, not least that doughty critic of a past era, Robert Lynd. Wide reading, desirable for all homilists, is imperative for those aspiring to use literature as a practical aid for preaching.

I feel it is important to include some thoughts about the ordained homilist's spirituality, and therefore seek vindication for doing so from various sources, St Augustine via Stephen Langton to the Second Vatican Council! And there is no escaping that 'liminality' factor (earlier mentioned) in the execution of a homily, whether the source is 'sacred' or 'secular' scripture.

The final word is left to the poets Emily Dickinson and Siegfried Sassoon, encompassing in a few lines much that has taken my treatise many thousands to consider.

Notes

1. Heaney, S. *The Redress of Poetry: Oxford Lectures* (Faber & Faber, London, 1995), p. 141.
2. Francis, D., CSsR, in *Theology of Preaching: Essays on Vision and Mission in the Pulpit*, ed. G. Heille, OP (Melisaunde, London, 2001), p. 89.
3. Hendrie, R., *Go, Tell Them: Thoughts Towards a Theology of Preaching* (St Paul's Publishing, London, 2006).

PART I

Chapter 1

Analogues of Revelation

So Philip ran to him and asked: 'Do you understand what you are reading?' And he said: 'How can I, unless someone guides me?' (Acts 8:30–31)

In *Sacred Space,* Timothy Radcliffe, OP, has contributed an essay, 'The World shall come to Walsingham', which has influenced considerably the *status quaestionis* of my argument.[1] Without delay, therefore, I offer some of the points he has raised, as a basis for further forays into the part that literature may play within the structures of preaching:

'None of us,' he declares,

who is a native to this country can remember the years it took for us to learn to speak English. Slowly we found ourselves at home in our tongue. We learn to be at ease within the conversation of our family and friends. This is the greatest gift we receive, a language in which we can speak and hear love. Similarly, human history is the journey home, nesting ourselves within the conversation that is the Trinity, whose Word is made flesh in Jesus ... Our pilgrimage to the Kingdom is learning a language in which we can be new people, a language in which we can flourish and be free ... It took centuries of people struggling to put into word praise and rejection, victories and defeats, liberation and exile, before the language was ready to receive the Word made flesh. It took all those prophets and scribes, soldiers and farmers, husbands and wives, before the language was ready to be fertilized by the Spirit.

In the light of Fr Radcliffe's approach to the evolution of language under God, possibilities about its relevance to my own interest in the homiletic uses of literature began to emerge.

Radcliffe again:

> Jesus could no more have been born earlier, than one could expect a baby Shakespeare to write *Hamlet*. The gestation of the Word took centuries. And the Incarnation is not the end of the story. We are still learning how to be at home in God's Word. It is still stretching open our language, so that it may be capacious enough for God. God became flesh in our words, and we are still learning to be at home in his Word.

By now one was aware not only that here was a profound insight into the correlation of the development of words and their preparatory place in awaiting the advent of God's Word, but that this same insight, derived from a volume by Boyle, was both fresh and hugely stimulating.[2]

Radcliffe's essay continues:

> But the journey does not end there. The Word has been made flesh, but all the rest of history will be catching up with this event ... The Bible does not offer us a religious language in which to speak of God. But it does more than that. It invites us to converse with God, to enter into a conversation which stretches open our ways of talking.

It is the author's concept of words and conversation and (as we shall later see) of the writtenness of words or literature as something universally relevant to humanity, that lifts the whole purpose of language, from the

Christian standpoint, into a dynamic and forward-moving force.

In a persuasive collection of Dominican essays, Herbert McCabe, OP, is quoted as follows:

> Our language does not encompass but simply strains towards the mystery that we encounter in Christ ... The theologian uses a word by stretching it to breaking point, and it is precisely as it breaks that the communication, if any, is achieved.[3]

Another of the essays, by Vivian Boland, OP, focuses thus on the notion of 'conversation':

> All things have been created in the Word, through the Word, and for the Word, and all things hold together in the Word ... The original 'text' then is this Word, first known to us perhaps through the translation of it that we call creation, the same creation that forms the first chapter in the history of salvation. Within this view all human conversation, discourse or talk may be understood as an echo of an earlier, radically fundamental conversation, discourse, or expression ... Where our conversation is directly concerned with God it is not only an echo but has also the character of a response, a reply to something already spoken ... Wherever there is justice and wisdom in our relationships and in the conversations that sustain those relationships, we are echoing something that is true about the universe itself and about its origin in a source that is wise and loving. Human conversation, exchange and communication that are worthy of human beings echo that conversation, exchange and communication which Christians believe God to be. Thomas Aquinas once again encourages us in thinking along these lines, this time with his endorsement of a comment attributed to St Ambrose, that 'any truth, no matter by whom it is said, is from the Holy Spirit' ... When our conversation seeks to include

God explicitly, whether in theology, preaching or prayer, it necessarily has the character of a reply, a response to an earlier expression. It is no longer an echo of the eternal conversation but is a response to it, or better, a response within it. All our preaching, then, insofar as it is a preaching of the Word of God is within the conversation that Father and Son carry on in the Spirit. We live in Trinity.[4]

Fr Radcliffe, in his notable book, *What is the Point of Being a Christian?* writes:[5]

Our hope of Paradise is not about the triumph of some dumb force ... It is the ultimate and unimaginable victory of meaning. Our story begins with God speaking a word, and Creation comes to be. He says, 'Let there be light, and there was light.' He creates with what Maximus the Confessor called 'the immeasurable force of wisdom'.

The foregoing paragraph connects with two lovely passages, one biblical, the other musical. First is the personification of Wisdom (Proverbs 8:30–1): 'Then I was beside him, like a master-workman; and I was daily his delight, rejoicing before him always, rejoicing in his inhabited world and delighting in the sons of men.' Secondly, there is that memorable and glorious moment near the beginning of Haydn's *Creation*, where the composer expresses the creation of light with a dramatic *tutti* chord from the orchestra, making the welkin ring.

Radcliffe again:

To exist is not a brute fact. It is to be held in being by God's word. So understanding things is not imposing arbitrary meaning on them: it is getting in touch with the Creator who gives them existence. And ever since Adam named the animals, then we have had the vocation to share in the speaking of that word until it brings about the completion of

Creation, the Kingdom. Whenever we speak to and about each other, then we are either being God's partners in creation, or else trying to subvert it.

And the author succinctly sums up his affirmation: 'The Word of God does not come down from heaven like a celestial Esperanto: it wells up from within human language. The birthpangs of the Word started when the first human beings began to speak.'[6]

Moving even closer to what will lie at the heart of this reflection, Radcliffe affirms that we are

forever searching for words that will let us delight in the particular and reach out to the universal. The movement that we saw beginning in the Old Testament, and finding its culmination in the New, carries on. We go on searching for words that are precise enough for the particularity of Jesus and spacious enough for his universality.

That is an approach thoughtfully put forward by Nicholas Boyle too, and will require further consideration ere long.[7]

Radcliffe then introduces a reflection which is key to the interconnection between preaching and literature: 'We have to learn the language of delight', we read, 'taking pleasure not just in Jesus but in each other.' He goes on: 'One of the ways in which we do so is through reading literature ... Literature opens our eyes to God's pleasure in his creatures.'

Then, widening his comments towards the Arts in general, he adds:

Our preaching of the Kingdom requires the renewal of our language by poets and artists. Not every preacher is a poet, but we need language that is kept alive, electric, tense and vibrant by poets. And that is a profound reason for the crisis of preaching today ... If the preaching of the word of God is to flourish, then we need poets and artists, singers and musicians who keep alive that intuition of our ultimate destiny. The Church needs these singers of the transcendent to nurture her life and her preaching.[8]

Nicholas Boyle argues strongly not only that the Bible is literature, but that literature is scripture (within Chapter 9, 'A Catholic Approach to Literature'). He writes:

A book becomes literature by using language for the purposeless purpose of enjoyment. But language is the medium of the Law, of the Word that tells us everything matters, even the sparrows on the rooftops. By showing life as mattering, and thus sharing in the work of the Spirit, literature enables us to take pleasure in a truth about human existence: the truth that its constitution is inescapably moral.[9]

We shall soon examine Boyle's position more, starting with his definition of literature, so crucial to his own argument and to the body of this argument. Before that, however, we will stay with Radcliffe to see first how gloriously wide his range and concept of literature is.[10] 'If we are taught to delight in people,' he says,

then we learn to see them as God sees them, even if the novelist or poet is not a believer. For George Mackay Brown, however, his poetry was profoundly part of his relationship with God. Even though he lived alone, he held that 'everyone is the writer's concern. The whole of humanity is his family and he must participate in their joys and ennuis and sufferings, otherwise what he does would be as meaningless as an endless game of patience.'

No precise locus is given from that snippet from the poet's letters, but its sentiments are in accord with the analysis of his work and character in Maggie Fergusson's fine biography.[11] Indeed Mackay Brown's philosophy was in tune with the dictum of the Roman playwright Terence: *Homo sum, humani nil a me alienum puto* ('I am a man; I count nothing human indifferent to me').[12]

Literature, then, is seen to sustain, as it were, the momentum of God's word. It homes in on the particular, and takes pleasure in what Louis MacNeice calls 'the drunkenness of things being various'.[13] Gerard Manley Hopkins, speaking of God in the lovely sonnet, *Pied Beauty*, spiritualized the same concept: 'He fathers forth whose beauty is past change: Praise him.'

MacNeice's image finds fuller development in an excerpt from a book called *The Grace and Task of Preaching*. Our author is Paul Murray, OP, and he writes:

> In a lengthy but illuminating work entitled *Treatise on the Formation of Preachers*, composed by the medieval Dominican, Blessed Humbert of Romans, there is one line, one phrase, which leaps off the page – at least for me. Humbert writes: 'I became like a man who is drunk, like someone sodden with wine, from my encounter with the words of God.'[14]

Murray continues:

> That image of drinking or of being made drunk is worth noting, for it is – I discovered a few years ago – an image which recurs over and over again in the writings of the early Dominican preachers, and not only in their theological writings and homilies but also in the stories they liked to tell about themselves. The image had been used before, of

course, by other religious traditions within the Church in order to evoke aspects of the spiritual and apostolic life. But Dominicans seem to have taken to this metaphor with a unique enthusiasm! In their conversations and homilies and writings, the image of drinking or of being made drunk described not only the overwhelming impact of the Word of God made on their interior lives, but also the effect of that encounter on almost every other aspect of their lives as preachers ... Humbert suggests that it is not always because of the preacher's own holiness or spiritual enthusiasm that the words of a particular homily catch fire, but rather because of the enthusiasm and awakened faith of God's people listening to the Word. It is because of them – the listeners – that the preacher is sometimes able, even while preaching, to enter into the fire of the Word.

Humbert quotes Proverbs (11:25): 'He who makes others drunk will himself be made drunk too.' And then he comments: 'The one who makes himself drunk with the words of God will himself be made drunk with a draught of manifold blessings.'[15]

W. H. Auden's clerihew about St Dominic's famous spiritual son may be pardonably inserted here:

> St Thomas Aquinas
> Always regarded wine as
> A medicinal juice
> That helped him to deduce.[16]

Returning to Radcliffe and his *Tablet* article, he tells of having experienced an immense variety of the world's literatures during his travels as Master General of his Order. 'This,' he avows, 'opens us up just a little more to the spaciousness of the Kingdom, the vastness of God.' That point is a strong one, helpful to preachers who consider that literature as a practical aid is not merely desirable, but theologically sustainable too. Radcliffe concludes: 'So it is not just that Christianity can express itself within these literatures. They deepen our sense of what it might mean to be part of Christ, in whom there is neither Jew nor Gentile, male nor female, slave nor free.' And I am left with this literary conundrum: when Hamlet, in answer to Polonius's query, 'What do you read, my Lord?' replies, 'Words, words, words', is the Bard implying a great deal more than meets the ear? I wonder.

We must look practically now at Boyle.[17] His definition of literature is this: 'Literature is language free from instrumental purpose, and it seeks to tell the truth'. 'These,' he declares,

> are the twin premises of a Catholic approach to literature, whether sacred or secular . . . It is helpful too that sacred and secular literature are in this way jointly marked off from what Paul Ricoeur calls ordinary and scientific discourse, which are seen as unselfconscious applications of a language that is for its users simply a medium of purposeful communication . . . It is the distinguishing mark of secular literature that it exploits writing in order to give pleasure, to entertain . . . Secular literary discourse sets out not to communicate or record information but simply to give pleasure in the written medium . . . As writtenness increases, as literature moves further away from communicative and purposive orality, so the element of play in it becomes more explicit and more 'philosophical'.[18]

And certainly Boyle's approach gains in persuasiveness in his examination of three quite disparate works – *Faust*, *Moby-Dick* and *Mansfield Park*!
   He further argues:

We enter fully into the realm of play, however, when we
arrive at poetry in the broad, Aristotelian sense . . . Here we
find whole works that have as their primary intention simply
to give pleasure in writtenness, by narrative and dramatic
representations of fictitious events, for example, or by the
measured expression of thought and feeling in verse.
However noble the conceptions of poetry, however
passionate or distressing the incidents it relates, they are all
put into words as the fulfilment of an intention to
entertain . . .[19]

Interestingly, the views of three past masters in this
field are at one with that of Boyle. First, Aristotle: 'From
childhood men have an instinct for representation
(*mimesis*), and in this respect man differs from the other
animals in that he is far more imitative and learns his first
lessons by representing things. And then there is the
enjoyment people always get from representations.'[20]
Secondly, Horace: 'I would advise one who has learned
the imitative art (*doctum imitatorem*) to look to life and
manners as a model, and draw from thence living
words.'[21] Thirdly, Hamlet's advice to the players: 'The
purpose of playing, whose end both at the first and now,
was and is to hold, as 'twere, the mirror up to nature.'[22]
  'That is the glory of poetry,' Boyle suggests, 'and of
secular literature generally, that out of such slight
material as the pleasure to be had from the weaving
together of words, it can make analogues of revelation
that can illuminate and affect the whole of our life.' What
a startling insight! If true, it would bring the entire
enterprise of using literature in preaching within a new
sphere of theological respectability.
  Boyle pursues his theme:

Literature, I think, shows us in words the truth about life. That is not its defining feature, for the defining feature of literature is its non-instrumental use of words, and the defining feature of secular literature is its non-instrumental use of words to give enjoyment. But if we deny the words literature uses to tell us truths about things, about individual beings, natural, personal, or cultural, we shall have great difficulty explaining how they tell us the truth about Being in general, how they amount, or are capable of amounting, to a Revelation.[23]

Undaunted by Professor Boyle's foray into Metaphysics, I am much indebted to him for the light he has shed about literature's legitimacy as a handmaid of Scripture. The thrust of his views has made it possible to argue more strongly for the practical role that literature may play within the homiletic discipline. The bulk of his reflections have been seminally part of my personal convictions over many years, and have happily compelled me to systematize my own thought upon sacred and secular scriptures.

Confronting the problem about the pleasure to be derived from tragedy, Boyle follows Aristotle's opinion that we take pleasure in the representation itself, and maintains that:

The pleasure we take in tragedy is pleasure in the consolation that is the sharing of grief and horror ... Moreover, what we share is not simply the emotional reaction to a fiction. It is the emotional reaction to a truth which the fiction has expressed. We share the pain of knowing a truth about our shared condition.[24]

Another aspect, this, of the 'mirror up to nature' syndrome already noted.

Moreover, Professor Boyle's assessment is reassuring in homiletic terms, enabling preachers to see the appropriateness of using literature to point up Jesus' horrific experiences throughout his Passion. This can be done without detracting in any way from the force of the Gospel narrative itself.

John Orme Mills, OP, another contributor to the volume *The Grace and Task of Preaching*, sustains the argument thus:

> As every good preacher well knows, in people's private lives there is in fact all too often quite a lot of tragedy – quite a lot of injustice and violence and loss – and if preaching consistently avoids these disturbing themes, the preachers will entertain, amuse or comfort the hearers, but will not touch on the deepest concerns of many of them. In fact, the preaching will not be conveying to them the message of Jesus Christ ... So it is part of the task of preachers to say something, at least at times, about the tragic side of the human condition. Play that down, and the victory of Christ will seem something remote from people's lives.[25]

As Virgil, in a wholly other context, ruminated: *Sunt lacrimae rerum, et mentem mortalia tangunt* ('There are tearful aspects to life, and human concerns affect the spirit').[26]

Boyle applies similar criteria, *mutatis mutandis*, to comedy, invoking Dickens, and Chesterton's opinions on Dickens, to ram home his point. My only hesitation in embracing the entire Dickensian corpus arises out of his propensity to champion, quite properly, the rights of the poor and underprivileged of his day (those imprisoned for debt, say). It is hard to see how parts of *Hard Times* or *The Old Curiosity Shop*, for instance, can be regarded as wholly non-purposive. Still, Boyle accepts the Chestertonian view about the art of Dickens and, in the light of it, makes this profound assertion: 'You cannot enjoy everybody unless they matter to you as they matter to themselves and to each other – unless, in other words, you can say of them what the Word of God said of the creation of the human race: "Behold, it was very good."'[27] Such a quasi-cosmic attitude to the place of literature in life is at one with Radcliffe's, and with my own, argument.

It has been argued that a book becomes literature by using language for what Boyle calls 'the purposeless purpose of enjoyment'. Thereafter, in scholarly fashion, he develops his ideas about the things that matter in life. The intensity of his writing, and its complexity, remind one somehow of the thick orchestration of a Brahms symphony. At any rate, his central theme is:

> By showing life as mattering, and thus sharing in the work of the Spirit, literature enables us to take that pleasure in a truth about human existence: the truth that its constitution is inescapably moral ... The pleasure Aristotle rightly says we take in representation, in the mere imitation of things, is the secular analogue of Redemption. Representation is the moral reality of Redemption projected into the secular realm of pleasure. Representation affirms – more, it enacts – the worth to God of what is represented.[28]

It has been affirming to meet this powerful view, a heady but telling admixture of Greek philosophy, persuasive deduction and religious thought.

Boyle proceeds:

> Because works of literature are made out of language, out of the original symbolic exercise of my pre-original

responsibility for my neighbour, they have at their heart a principled universality which fits them to participate symbolically in that interaction of Law and loss and reconciliation which Christians call Atonement or Redemption ... That it (fiction) tells us many truths, that it is, as we say, true to life, is the guarantee of its veracity, the guarantee that the world of this text is a part of the world we know and inhabit: and it shares with us what we share with one another.[29]

A Catholic homilist whose practice is to use literature as an aid cannot but be reassured by Boyle's statement, and come to realize fearlessly that authors of all sorts, Christian or not, may have a legitimate role in the elucidation of biblical texts.

Boyle again:

What supreme works of literature reveal is, therefore, not some ultimate and homogeneous eternal moment, but the permanent interaction of Law, judgement and reconciliation which is the source of existence insofar as it is open to us to know it. The revelation at the heart of secular literature is in the deepest sense a moral revelation, and therefore it is a revelation of God. Perhaps in the end all I am saying is that if we believe the teachings of the Catholic Church to be true statements about human life, then we must necessarily expect literature that is true to life to reflect and corroborate them, whether or not it is written by Catholics.[30]

An acceptable summation, that, for any Catholic priest, litterateur or not! We need not say more at this point about Boyle's subsequent reflections, with some of which Chapter Six will deal – except for this: in response to the question where this secular revelation stops, he replies:

Sacred and secular literature may make use of the same, or some of the same genres, they may even at times share similar subject-matter, but the limit defining – putting the end to – the area of overlap between them is provided by the imperative form: 'Thou shalt.' Secular literature can go so far as to show us life lived under the sway of the commandment, it can let us glimpse Being modified by primordial obligation . . . but it cannot utter the commandment itself, for it does not have the authority . . . The genres used in sacred literature may take it far inside the territory of secularity . . . but it always retains the formal relation to commandment which marks the frontier with secularity . . . Secular scriptures, in short, are the way in, the prolegomena, to the sacred scriptures. They provide the commentary that makes the original text accessible, the atmosphere of application, elaboration and response that the written law needs in order to breathe and live.[31]

As a homilist I have always felt with passion, and still do, that the appropriate accompaniment of secular literature (in particular, poetry) can indeed 'provide the commentary that makes the original [biblical] text accessible'.

Seamus Heaney describes a poem by Dylan Thomas as giving 'the sensation of language on the move toward a destination in knowledge'. He writes: 'We go to poetry, we go to literature in general, to be forwarded within ourselves. The best it can do is to give us an experience that is like foreknowledge of certain things which we already seem to be remembering.'[32] It is almost as if the spirit of Wordsworth and his *Ode on the Intimations of Immortality* were haunting the Irish poet. Tennyson, in the octave of one of his sonnets, apparently ponders similarly:

As when with downcast eyes we muse and brood,
And ebb into a former life, or seem
To lapse far back in a confused dream
To states of mystical similitude;
If one but speaks or hems or stirs his chair,
Ever the wonder waxeth more and more,
So that we say, 'All this hath been before,
All this hath been, I know not when or where.'[33]

Nicholas Boyle's conclusion in his inspiring chapter, 'A Catholic Approach to Literature', spiritedly recalls a recurring theme: 'Even in the works and words that seem to hide God's face or to spit on it, we can see God revealed at the heart of our world and in our culture.'[34]

Fr Martin Boland (Catholic chaplain at the University of Essex) adds a rider in an article in *The Tablet* (23 June 2007) thus:

Within Catholic thought, there is a long-held appreciation that art, whether sacred or profane, can express something of what Hans Urs von Balthasar describes as the glory of being and the mystery of Otherness. Serious artistic expressions will always have human and divine bite.

As with art, so with literature.

The glory of being and the mystery of Otherness was a concern of the late Welsh clergyman-poet, R. S. Thomas – now certain, now vulnerable in his believing. Contrast, for instance, the conclusion in *The Answer*:

There have been times
when, after long on my knees
in a cold chancel, a stone has rolled
from my mind, and I have looked

> in and seen the old questions lie
> folded and in a place
> by themselves, like the piled
> graveclothes of love's risen body.[35]

And, in *Where?*:

> Where to turn without turning
> To stone? From the one side
> history's Medusa stares,
> from the other one love
> on its cross. While the heart
> fills not with light
> from the mind, but with the shadow
> too much of such light casts.[36]

Boyle and Radcliffe have confirmed notions of mine previously held about the place and purpose of a literary input for preaching. At times their insights have brought on an Archimedean *eureka* or a Keatsian frisson like that of 'stout Cortez' and his men. Beyond that, however, I have been led to feel, as Gerard Manley Hopkins did in his youthful *Let me be to Thee as the circling bird*:

> I have found the dominant of my range and state –
> Love, O my God, to call Thee Love and Love.[37]

In the remainder of this reflection, I hope, through an admixture of the academic and the autobiographical, to show how literature may indeed be a practical aid to preaching, for literature 'is language free of instrumental purpose, and it seeks to tell the truth'.

In the next chapter I shall examine the role of 'secular

literature' in preaching in the light of my personal experience as Spiritual Director to the students of the Scots College in Rome and of my earlier years as a producer of religious programmes with the BBC.

Notes

1. Radcliffe, T., OP, 'The World Shall Come to Walsingham', in *Sacred Space: House of God, Gate of Heaven*, ed. P. North and J. North (Continuum, London, 2007), pp. 65–79.
2. Boyle, N., *Sacred and Secular Scriptures: A Catholic Approach to Literature* (Darton, Longman, and Todd, London, 2004), pp. 125–45. (The author is most grateful to Professor Boyle for giving his blessing to quote him so extensively.)
3. McCabe, H., in *The Grace and Task of Preaching*, ed. M. Monshau (Dominican Publications, Dublin, 2006), p. 121.
4. Boland, V., in *Grace and Task of Preaching*, pp. 61–2, 64.
5. Radcliffe, T., *What is the Point of Being a Christian?* (Continuum, London, 2005), p. 17.
6. Radcliffe, p. 79.
7. Boyle, pp. 134–5.
8. Radcliffe, in *Grace and Task of Preaching*, pp. 122–3.
9. Boyle, p. 132.
10. Radcliffe, 'Literature as Scripture', *The Tablet* (26 May 2007), p. 15.
11. Fergusson, M., *George Mackay Brown: The Life* (John Murray, London, 2006), *passim*.
12. Terence, *Heauton Timorumenos*, I, 1.
13. MacNeice, L., *The Collected Poems of Louis MacNeice*, 'Snow', ed. E. R. Dodds (Faber & Faber, London, 1966), p. 30.
14. Murray, P., in *Grace and Task of Preaching*, pp. 224–7.
15. 'Treatise on the formation of preachers, no. 70', in *Early Dominicans: Selected Writings*, ed. S. Tugwell, (Paulist Press, New York, 1982), p. 195.
16. Auden, W.H., *Academic Graffiti* (Faber and Faber, London, 1971), p. 2.
17. Boyle, ch. 9, *passim*.
18. Boyle, pp. 125, 126.

19. Boyle, p. 127.
20. Aristotle, *Poetics*, iii, 4.
21. Horace, *Ars Poetica*, 317-8.
22. *Hamlet*, Act III, 2, 22.
23. Boyle, p. 128.
24. Boyle, p. 130.
25. Mills, J. O., OP, in *Grace and Task of Preaching*, pp. 315-6.
26. Virgil, *Aeneid*, I, 462.
27. Boyle, p. 132.
28. Boyle, pp. 132-3.
29. Boyle, p. 139.
30. Ibid.
31. Boyle, pp. 141, 142.
32. Heaney, *Redress of Poetry*, pp. 141, 159.
33. 'As when with downcast eyes we muse and brood', in *A Century of Sonnets: The Romantic-era Revival, 1750-1850*, ed. P. R. Feldman and D. Robinson (Oxford University Press, US, 1999), p. 193.
34. Boyle, p. 145.
35. Thomas, R. S., *Collected Poems 1945-1990* (Phoenix Giant, London, 1993), p. 59.
36. Ibid., p. 520.
37. *Poems of Gerard Manley Hopkins*, ed. W. H. Gardner (Oxford University Press, London, 1964), p. 37.

Chapter 2

Strands of Experience:
broadcasting and seminary

And gladly wolde he learn, and gladly teche.[1]

In the previous chapter, having investigated the meaning and the interrelationship of 'sacred' and 'secular' scripture, in this one I will seek to examine their roles through two sets of personal experience: first, my time as a producer with the BBC, and second, my years as Spiritual Director of the Pontifical Scots College in Rome. The former was concerned entirely with the use and communication of words, while the latter brought with it the happy duty of preparing and training gifted students for the ministry of preaching.

These lines in one of St Augustine's sermons may be appropriate here:

> If I think of what I want to say, the word is already in my heart. And if I want to talk to you, I look for some means whereby what is in my heart may also be in yours. So, wanting the word which is already in my heart to come over to you, and make its way into your heart, I make use of my voice to talk to you. The sound of the voice brings you to understand the word. And when my voice has done this, it ceases; but the word carried to you by the sound is now already in your heart and has not left mine.[2]

The appointment to the BBC's Religious Department in Glasgow came in 1969. The interviewing panel seemed to look kindly upon my interest in drama, public speaking, teaching and literature, and their opening question was as searching as it was pertinent: 'How would you assess the difference between the television viewers of today and the experience of those viewing the images in the cave in Plato's *Republic?*' Mercifully, part of Book 7 of that work was read by my Greek class in Edinburgh under D. J. Allan some twenty years before, and memory came sufficiently to the rescue.

The Religious Department was led by Dr Ronnie Falconer, who saw to it that his team was close-knit and ecumenical. Hence from time to time one's efforts were channelled towards a wide variety of programmes involving broadcasters from several traditions.

There was much to learn and much to appreciate, not least on the preaching side. To encounter some of its finest exponents was exciting. Though by now elderly, James S. Stewart, Leonard Small, George McLeod, Archie Craig and the inimitable William Barclay came regularly to the microphone. From the Catholic fold Cardinal Gordon Gray stood out, as did two maverick Dominicans, Anthony Ross and Columba Ryan.

The extent and manner of contributors' use of literature was inevitably diverse. It was up to the producers to enable and encourage them and, wherever the script seemed to require improvement, to persuade rather than compel. The proportion of well-read clergy was high, so the use of 'secular scripture' was generally neither precious nor obtrusive.

Staff were sometimes required to broadcast, testingly, on 'live' transmissions like *Thought for the Day* or

Lighten our Darkness. Such homiletic skills as we had were helpful; for even where the programme was intimate, not liturgical, the demands of clarity, pace and conviction were unremitting.

It could fall to a producer (usually at short notice) to take a church or studio service. I recall the late arrival of a poor script for the World Service and Dr Falconer's insisting that I sit down and replace it at once. It was one within a series on the Seven Deadly Sins, 'gluttony' on this occasion, and I based my sudden reflections upon certain lines of the Defendant in Gilbert and Sullivan's *Trial by Jury*:

> You cannot eat breakfast all day,
> Nor is it the act of a sinner,
> When breakfast is taken away,
> To turn your attention to dinner;
> And it's not in the range of belief,
> That you could hold him as a glutton,
> Who, when he is tired of beef,
> Determines to tackle the mutton.

Transmissions of Mass in those days were 'live', Reformed services being normally pre-recorded. 'Live' situations heightened the sense of immediacy. 'Feature' programmes were scheduled from time to time, and this meant working now and again with professional actors, whose interpretation of literary extracts was expert. My final radio production, in 1977, had Lennox Milne reading her favourite poems. An aspiring homilist would have seen what a wonderful vehicle poetry can be for conveying truth, beauty and love through words, or, if you will, for supplying 'secular' literary aid to the 'sacred' content of Holy Writ. Again let it be stressed what a key role literature can have in the soul's pursuit of the truth.

My duties in Rome began in the autumn of 1977, my chief task being to be the confidant of some fifty students preparing for the Catholic priesthood. External commitments (as opposed to the confidential work of the 'internal forum') included the oversight of the homiletic programme – an experience at once stimulating and humbling. I was required too to give a weekly talk on some spiritual topic to each year-group, from newcomers to senior theologians. Their competence in the use of English varied hugely, according to the quality of their earlier education and the breadth of their general reading. Openness to the riches not only of literature but also of music and art cannot but make for a more civilized person and, *pari passu*, a more cultured priest. Rome was the perfect setting and stimulus.

Unsurprisingly, literature found a place in my talks, less in the spirit of a manic crusade than of a desire that the seminarians be 'surprised by joy' in their encounters with great writing, which, we recall from Boyle, is 'language free from instrumental purpose, and it seeks to tell the truth'. I had a tally of nearly seven hundred talks over an eight-year period (some favourite topics having more than one airing). I would keep a hopeful eye upon the homiletic by-products that these addresses might engender. I was constantly hoping that for some students at least there might be a convergence of sacred and secular scriptures which could affect their approach to the preaching apostolate.

Within the talks I would sometimes include a complete poem (some of George Herbert's, *The Pulley* and

Redemption among them, being especially attractive), and try to elicit responses arising out of the lines' loveliness. Hymns and canticles were a problem, the finest tending to be in Latin, with many translations on the weak side. Still, thirty years ago many students had a modicum of Latin vocabulary, and outstanding pieces like *Lauda Sion*, composed by Thomas Aquinas for the festival of Corpus Christi, the Marian *Ave, maris stella*, the *Dies Irae* for Requiem Masses, and the martial *Vexilla Regis* (sung on Holy Thursday) were sufficiently understood. The first-mentioned is a splendid synthesis of refined Latin and Eucharistic theology for which the plainchant setting is sublime. Phrases or single lines (translated) can profitably be inserted into a homily in a parish liturgy.

Self-indulgence is always a danger for the litterateur. All I could attempt to do was to provide the soil, as it were, in which the students could, if they wished, grow their own literary flora. Long works had as a rule to be excluded. *Paradise Lost* (which I waded right through one summer vacation as a student), replete as it is with 'purple patches', was dispensed only in titbits! It is unlikely that any student, setting himself to read that epic entire, would have shared the excitement Keats felt on first looking into Chapman's Homer!

Among shorter works I loved to range widely, in the spirit of Montaigne (*Essais* 3,12): 'I have gathered a posy of other men's flowers, and of my own I have only provided the string that ties them together.' Moreover, since spirituality cannot be fashion's slave, the flowers have been plucked from all manner of nooks in the garden.

There can be an engaging affinity between the tenor of varied periods and styles. For example, in my talk entitled *Trapped*, I began with Dorothy Parker's quaint assertion: 'There was I, trapped like a trap in a trap' (sic), and linked it to three disparate pieces: *The Snare*, by the Irish poet James Stephens; *Reynard the Fox*, by John Masefield; and Shakespeare's *Venus and Adonis*. Each has its poignant element of fear, impending doom and helplessness. Homiletically, an understanding chord could be struck with an anxious listener. The fact that the poets narrate the distress of terrified animals, not human beings, in no way invalidates that point. Francis of Assisi, Martin de Porres and kindred souls would surely concur.

Nicholas Boyle deals philosophically with the problems inherent in Herman Melville's *Moby-Dick*, the tale of Captain Ahab's manic whale-hunt. '*Moby-Dick*,' he asserts,

> is undoubtedly a wicked book. The challenge for a Catholic reader of the book is to find out whether, or how far, Melville was right to feel as untouched by that wickedness as Christ, the lamb, by the sin he came to forgive – whether, or how far, the book itself embodies that redemptive purity. *Moby-Dick* is in one sense the story of Faust carried to its logical or illogical extreme – a rejection of Christ and a pact with the Devil which takes the Devil fully seriously.[3]

Set against such depth of insight, my three poems may seem of trivial account, though perhaps those of us who burrow away in the lowlier foothills of literary endeavour may gaze with fraternal recognition at Boyle and his peers on their literary Everest.

Gerard Manley Hopkins, a favourite poet, would often feature in my talks. His technique was not a chief concern. Enthusing over 'inscape' or 'sprung rhythm' might have scared my flock off him for life. What did concern me was the application of his ideas and insights to their present and future lives as priests and preachers.

The simplicity of some of his early poems often surprised the seminarians (*Easter*, for instance, or *Rosa Mystica*), though I tried to show them how the poet's inspiration developed from year to year (say in *Heaven-Haven* or *Winter with the Gulf Stream*). The latter exhibits the kind of natural image the author would later perfect, with touches transferable to spiritual experience, for example:

> A simple passage of weak notes
> Is all the winter bird dare try.[4]

I had to tread cautiously, restraining my urge to rhapsodize over the glories of *The Wreck of the Deutschland*, especially stanzas 12–23 with their account of the storm. However, the students seemed to cope with some of the later sonnets, elements of despair and all, together with *The Blessed Virgin compared to the Air we breathe*, devotionally and homiletically so deep. Its century of iambic trimeters contains some figurative devices of great strength, as in the opening lines:

> Wild air, world-mothering air,
> Nestling me everywhere,
> That each eyelash or hair
> Girdles; goes home betwixt
> The fleeciest, frailest-fixed
> Snowflake . . .[5]

Putting such writings in the context of authors' lives was valuable. Hopkins' interior struggles make more sense then to a perplexed reader: thus we appreciate the driving asceticism of *The Habit of Perfection* on the one hand, and his compassionate pastoral care in *Felix Randal* on the other hand. I tried to find a link between the poet's personal battles and those the students themselves might meet in their own lives or the lives of others later on. These lines, from sonnet no. 70, I begged them to consider carefully:

> Natural heart's ivy, Patience masks
> Our ruins of wrecked past purpose.[6]

Pastorally that might accompany a homily-text, or even substitute for one, or if it were felt to be 'above the heads' of parishioners, the priest himself could hold it as a stimulus. There is balm in those words for wearied or worried souls.

To avoid engaging in literary criticism and not in preaching, I will quote a passage from the Foreword to Pope Benedict XVI's recently published *Jesus of Nazareth*: 'Neither the individual books of Holy Scripture nor the Scripture as a whole are simply a piece of literature. The Scripture emerged from within the heart of a living subject – the pilgrim People of God – and lives within this same subject.'[7]

The Holy Father is implicitly acknowledging that Scripture is itself literature (though not primarily so), and that its roots are within the heart of the People of God, that is, the Church. The fitting role of general literature must then be to widen and interpret for the Church's members, through 'holding the mirror up to Nature', ways in which their pilgrimage may fruitfully proceed. A shade more earthily, Professor Boyle:

> My pleasure in the shape of the tulip, for example, is disinterested – not, as Nietzsche would have it, because of some effete lack of will on my part, but because I envisage everyone else as sharing it, and that universality is not compatible with any one-sided exploitation of the tulip for my own benefit. How much more must this argument apply to the pleasure I take in literary composition, which is a human, not a natural, work and which is constructed in the very medium of communication, in language?[8]

The thing of beauty, therefore, is a joy for ever (*pace* Keats).

A Catholic poet of our own time whose faith and whose delight in natural beauty shone through was George Mackay Brown, who lived and wrote almost exclusively in Orkney. As with Hopkins, however, so with Brown, the sadder sides of life are often apparent. The piece I most shared with the students was his *The Funeral of Ally Flett*. The pathos expressed over the death of that young tearaway is intense. What escape is there for young folk from drink, drugs and recklessness? A pastoral matter is sensitively treated, and this is an extract:

> Because the hour of grass is brief
> And the red rose
> Is a bare thorn in the east wind
> And a strong life
> Runs out and spends itself like barren sand
> And the dove dies
> And every loveliest lilt must have a close,
> Old Betsy came with bitter cries.[9]

The whole poem could arguably be read – perhaps to replace a homily – at a Requiem for a youngster similarly trapped. Scripture readings, appropriately chosen, would have to come first.

'Heavyweights' between Hopkins and Brown were discussed too: Francis Thompson (notably his masterpiece *The Hound of Heaven*), G. K. Chesterton and Hilaire Belloc. Let a snippet from each of them show the homiletic impact deducible from masterly versification. Thompson, in his *Kingdom of God*, stresses God's nearness to us in our daily experience, along lines developed later by Teilhard de Chardin:

> The drift of pinions, would we hearken,
> Beats at our own clay-shuttered doors.[10]

Chesterton ends one of his earliest poems, *A Prayer in Darkness* with words that might help out a children's homily on the Passion:

> Men say the sun was darkened, yet I had
> Thought it beat brightly, even on – Calvary;
> And he that hung upon the torturing tree
> Heard all the crickets singing, and was glad.[11]

Belloc's prayer, *Ballade to Our Lady of Czestochowa*, concludes hauntingly with a devotional Marian thought:

> You shall receive me when the clouds are high
> With evening, and the sheep attain the fold.[12]

In lighter vein, I would use the same author's apt epigram in my introductory talk to first-year students:

> Kings live in palaces, and pigs in sties,
> And youth in expectation. Youth is wise.[13]

With other Christian poets I travelled far afield, going with homiletic intent to authors as diverse in time and approach as the Scots William Dunbar and William Drummond; the nineteenth-century ladies Christina Rossetti and Emily Dickinson; or the Jesuit martyr Robert Southwell and another Catholic, Richard Crashaw. No one could surpass the latter's brilliant epigram about the miracle at Cana: *Nympha pudica Deum vidit, et erubuit*, for which his own translation ran: 'The shame-faced water saw its Lord, and blushed.' Not that I urged the inclusion of Latin in a homily, save in the case of academics or monks!

I generally eschewed contemporary poetry, though a few tried favourites cropped up in my talks and homilies: certain things by R. S. Thomas[14] (*The Empty Church* or *Flowers*, for instance), Ted Hughes[15] (especially from his volume *Remains of Elmet*), Norman MacCaig[16] (short pieces such as *Assisi*), and a powerful piece by Geoffrey Hill,[17] a testimonial to the heroism of Dietrich Bonhoeffer.

Special among Eastern influences were Edward Fitzgerald's translation of the *Rubaiyat of Omar Khayyam*, described by the editors of *The English Parnassus* as 'the language's most finished expression of the spirit's darker broodings, its most searching music in the minor key'. This quatrain may serve as a homiletic aperitif:

> The moving finger writes; and, having writ,
> Moves on: nor all thy Piety and Wit
> Shall lure it back to cancel half a Line,
> Nor all thy Tears wash out a Word of it.[18]

Too pretentious for parish usage? Not, I think, if well read and linked intelligibly to the Scripture or topic of the time. If we worry too much about the level of our hearers' intelligence we may do two things: condescend, or find ourselves obliged to omit much of the Old Testament from our preaching remit. Sacred and secular scriptures alike demand scholarship and insight for precise interpretation; they also demand a sufficiency of common sense and presentational skills if they are to be effectively preached.

Literature in general and poetry in particular would, I hoped, be not only a practical aid for the homilist, but also for the personal and collective benefit of all of us within the College community. A quest for individual holiness and a spirit of service to others – chiefly attainable through prayer and good works – might be stimulated by memorable lines, and, in turn, they might enhance the force and beauty of the Bible message. Sacred and secular scriptures should relate to one another without ever jarring.

The above reference to the personal and collective benefit that literature could bestow suggests that the latter would focus upon lines (prose or verse) affording encouragement to the student body reflecting and praying together, whereas the former would depend upon passages that might advance this or that student's private meditation or spiritual reading. In all such areas, however, I always insisted on the importance of freedom of choice, in the spirit of Terence's dictum: *Quot homines tot sententiae: suo quoque mos* ('So many men, so many opinions, his own a law to each'), in his *Phormio* (l. 454).

As it happened, a few favourites emerged for both

kinds. On the personal side were the Shepherd's Song, compellingly simple, from *The Pilgrim's Progress*;[19] A. H. Clough's *Say not, the struggle nought availeth*, a model for fortitude;[20] and the Scots poet R. W. Buchanan's *Judas*, a ballad about temptation and forgiveness.[21] On the communal side, students responded positively as a rule to the war poets and the moral issues raised by them, Isaac Rosenberg and Wilfred Owen especially; whilst in the sphere of communication skills Robert Graves' *The Cool Web* was popular.[22] Its third stanza contains implicit advice for the clergy:

> There's a cool web of language winds us in,
> Retreat from too much joy or too much fear:
> We grow sea-green at last and coldly die
> In brininess and volubility.

Wordy preachers should beware. Even bishops are not immune. One priest told me that when a certain prelate preached he sensed a whiff of eternity, a premonition that the man would never end! Broadcasting was ruthless in this matter: over-run, and you will be taken off the air. Further, the use of literature assists the homilist from time to time by producing for his benefit more aptly and succinctly what he might have needed many words to say.

Prose works in support of that contention abound, but seem to centre around certain classic treatises of the past, like *The Imitation of Christ* (Thomas à Kempis), the anonymous *Cloud of Unknowing*, *Revelations of Divine Love* (Julian of Norwich), *The Ladder of Perfection* (Walter Hilton), and *Introduction to the Devout Life* (St Francis de Sales).

In the realm of drama, clearly Shakespeare was the

principal source, and I produced on stage parts of *Hamlet* and *Twelfth Night* with them. It also fell to me to present full-length dramas, including Jean Anouilh's *Antigone*, two by James Bridie and R. C. Sherriff's *Home at Seven*. Such Thespianism would have been a difficulty for Catholic clergy years before. At the time of my own ordination, one needed permission to set foot in a theatre. In a moment I shall look back at the sermon classes taken in the College. Given, however, the literary slant which I would encourage the students to consider, I wish to repeat this quotation from Professor Boyle:

> Secular scriptures in short are the way in, the prolegomena, to the sacred scriptures. They provide the commentary that makes the original text accessible, the atmosphere of application, elaboration, and response that the written law needs in order to breathe and live.[23]

Yet there is another, crucial dimension to keep in mind. It is expressed well by Fr Daniel O'Leary in *The Tablet* of 21 July 2007. He writes:

> All our teaching will be sterile until it springs from a full heart. Three times Jesus so tenderly drew out the fullness of Peter's thrice-denied love before entrusting to him the immense work of nourishing God's people. Only when Peter had his love for his great friend restored did Jesus feel that he was ready to teach. Mark Van Doren wrote a poem about the teacher he most remembered:
>
> > It must unfold as grace, inevitably, necessarily,
> > as tomcats stretch: in such a way he lolled upon
> >   his desk
> > and fell in love again before our very eyes
> > again, again – how many times again! –

with Dante, Chaucer, Shakespeare, Milton's Satan,
as if his shameless, glad, compelling love
were all he really wanted us to learn.[24]

Correlated with those lines, there occurs in the
Foreword to the recently published *John Henry Newman
in his Time* a quotation of some encouragement to
prospective preachers:

> Men live after their death – or still more they live not in
> their writings or their chronicled history, but in that
> *agraphos mneme* ('unwritten memory') exhibited in a school
> of pupils who trace their moral parentage to them. As moral
> truth is discovered not by reasoning, but by habituation, so
> it is recommended not by books, but by oral instruction.[25]

My sessions took place weekly in the College chapel
in term-time, and in no way resembled what
Shakespeare called 'sessions of sweet, silent thought'.
After all, this was a community of young, gifted and
forthright men, hailing mostly from the South-West of
Scotland, anxiously eager to learn, and sometimes
opinionated! Each was required to preach twice within
the academic year. It fell to me to oversee (some might
say to referee) the proceedings gently but firmly. The
basis for the preachments was readings from
the Lectionary (usually for Sundays). Ten minutes was
the maximum length.

I made myself available for consultation well in
advance, and a personal acquaintanceship with every
speaker led to an easy approach. The challenge was to
ensure that what was to be said was what the student
himself wanted to say rather than what I might wish to
hear. For students, for all of us who preach, may there be

no enslavement to other people's 'sermon-notes', let alone the Internet. I did try to avoid 'leaning' on the homilist in terms of style or content. Many toiled hard to prepare, and reminded me of the poet Horace's expression *limae labor et mora* ('the labour and delaying of the file').[26] Albert Nolan, OP, sees this particular challenge for anyone who wishes to preach effectively. 'It is,' he says, 'in the famous words of Thomas Aquinas, to see our preaching as *contemplata aliis tradere*, which we usually translate as "giving to others the fruits of our contemplation".'[27] The nature and intensity of the College's routine in the 1980s did enable the students to follow thoughtful spiritual routes. Actually the word *tradere* does not merely mean 'to give', but rather 'to hand over' something first given to us, in this case the Word. Whether and to what extent a student wished to 'hand over' secular as well as sacred scriptures in the process was a matter of his own choice. If asked for advice on the issue, I would try to work through the possibilities of this quotation or that allusion within the compass of his understanding and experience.

Two Shakespearean sayings featured in my advice: first, Hamlet's admonition: 'but if you mouth it (the speech), as many of your players do, I had as lief the town-crier spoke my line'; second, Berowne's attack on preciosity in *Love's Labour's Lost*:

> Taffeta phrases, silken terms precise,
> Three-piled hyperboles, spruce affectation,
> Figures pedantical.[28]

Happily, interest in such admonitions was only a part of a positive response by the students to the whole purpose of using literature as a practical aid to preaching.

The strict confidentiality attached to the duties of a Spiritual Director ceases when he is invited to deal with 'external' matters like homiletics. This one, believing, with Robert Frost, that 'poetry begins in delight and ends in wisdom'[29] hopes that his former students may have been enriched by the thoughts, words and sounds of poetry and other fine literature (secular scripture). I look back on those far-off days with joy, as sure now as I was then that 'well-ordered words are as a honeycomb, sweet to the soul and health to the bones'.[30] The whole homiletic endeavour was to work towards an increase, in ourselves and others, of holiness and culture. That last word's Latin root has two meanings, 'cultivation' and 'worship', though when it comes to spiritual growth each meaning has its relevance.

There is a significant quotation from the Vatican's *Pastoral Instruction on the Means of Social Communication*: transfer these remarks, *mutatis mutandis*, to our concern with secular scriptures, for reassurance and encouragement:

> It is a fact that when you writers and artists are able to reveal in the human condition, however lowly or sad it may be, a spark of goodness, at that very instant a glow of beauty pervades your whole work. We are not asking of you that you should play the part of moralists. We are only asking you to have confidence in your mysterious power of opening up the glorious regions of light that lie behind the mystery of man's life.[31]

'Opening up the glorious regions of light' through the use of 'sacred' and 'secular' literature was at the heart of my priestly task both in broadcasting and in the seminary, though in different ways. Such a task could only be undertaken in the light of the growth in literary appreciation which had accrued over the years. To look at some of the 'stimuli' behind that growth will be the aim of the ensuing chapter.

Notes

1. Chaucer, Prologue to the Canterbury Tales, (line 310) in *The English Parnassus: An Anthology Chiefly of Longer Poems* ed. W. Macneil Dixon & H.J.C. Grierson, Oxford 1921, 7.
2. Sermon 293, 3.
3. Boyle, p. 190.
4. *Poems of Gerard Manley Hopkins*, p. 23.
5. Ibid., p. 99.
6. Ibid., p. 110.
7. Pope Benedict XVI, *Jesus of Nazareth*, trans. Adrian J. Walker (Bloomsbury, London, 2007), Foreword.
8. Boyle, p. 129.
9. Brown, G. M., *The Year of the Whale* (John Murray, London, 1965), p. 10.
10. *Collected English Verse*, ed. R. and M. Bottrall (Sidgewick and Jackson, London, 1947), p. 496.
11. Goudge, E., *A Book of Comfort* (Collins, Glasgow, 1982), p. 241.
12. Belloc H., *Sonnets and Verse* (Duckworth, London, 1954), p. 136.
13. Ibid., p. 159.
14. Thomas, D., *Collected Poems*, pp. 349, 390.
15. Hughes, T., *Remains of Elmet* (Faber and Faber, London, 1979).
16. MacCaig, N., *Collected Poems* (Chatto and Windus, London, 1990), p. 155.
17. Hill, G., 'Tenebrae', in *Collected Poems* (Andre Deutsch, London, 1978), p. 41.
18. *The English Parnassus*, p. 748.
19. *Oxford Book of Christian Verse*, ed. D. Cecil (Clarendon Press, Oxford, 1941), p. 194.

20. Palgrave, F.T., Palgrave's *The Golden Treasury* (Oxford University Press, Oxford, 1914), p. 400.
21. *Oxford Book of Christian Verse*, pp. 488–91.
22. Graves, R., *Collected Poems* (Guild Publishing, London, 1975), p. 37.
23. Boyle, p. 142.
24. O'Leary, D., in *The Tablet* (21 July 2007).
25. *John Henry Newman in his Time*, ed. P. Lefebvre and C. Mason, (Family Publications, Oxford, 2007), Foreword.
26. Horace, *Ars Poetica*, 1291.
27. Nolan, A., OP, in *Grace and Task of Preaching*, p. 239.
28. Shakespeare, *Love's Labour's Lost*, IV, 2, 407.
29. Quoted in E. Albert, *History of English Literature* (Harrap, London, 1979), p. 458.
30. Proverbs 16:24.
31. Pontifical Commission for the Means of Social Communication, *Communio et Progressio*, 55.

Chapter 3

Stimuli

Your true lover of literature is never fastidious.[1]

Staying with the Boylian affirmation: 'Literature is language free of instrumental purpose, and it seeks to tell the truth', I now wish to turn to certain passages of prose and verse which have proved a potent influence in my own preaching and approach to preaching over the years. The selection is small, but hopefully representative, and bearing out the ideas discussed in the previous two chapters. 'Representation,' wrote Boyle,[2]

is the moral reality of Redemption projected into the secular realm of pleasure. Representation affirms – more, it enacts – the worth to God of what is represented. However appalling or dispiriting, however low or laughable, the life that is represented, sinful life just as it is, serving no further purpose but just being there – life as it is for its Maker and Redeemer – is affirmed by the act of representation to be worth the labour and love and attention that go into the showing it (by the artist) and the recognizing it (by the audience) ... The fictions of human individuality that we call characters, the fictions of human interaction that we call plots, the fictions of a meditating and soliloquizing human consciousness that we call (lyric) poetry – they all tell us or show us many truths about what people are like, about how they feel and behave, about what the world looks like to us and others.

Let us consider the following passages in the light of those remarks, and keep in mind how pastoral and practical material may be gleaned from them towards homiletic enrichment. Keats, Shaw, Thompson, Dickens, Hopkins and Duff Cooper (with an anonymous poem superadded) – a weighty though disparate amalgam yet, assembled together, capable of meeting our present requirements. The order of their selection reflects the different stages of my life when they were first encountered.

Keats was met first at school through (inevitably) the *Ode to Autumn*, but it was *The Eve of St Agnes* that entranced me more. The romantic tale opens with three evocative stanzas of rare beauty in which an old beadsman is pictured at prayer. The detail of the word-pictures and the touching imagery are superb: I give the opening lines:

> St Agnes' Eve – Ah, bitter chill it was!
> The owl, for all his feathers, was a-cold,
> The hare limp'd trembling through the frozen grass,
> And silent was the flock in woolly fold:
> Numb were the beadsman's fingers, while he told
> His rosary, and while his frosted breath,
> Like pious incense from a censer old,
> Seem'd taking flight for heaven, without a death,
> Past the sweet Virgin's picture, while his prayer he saith.[3]

The Spenserian stanzas, with their final hexameter line, help to establish the atmospheric solemnity of the story. Homiletically, our lines would befit not only the saint's feast-day (January 21st) but any wintertime liturgy.

Martyrs, especially child-martyrs, are properly recalled as sources of inspiration to the memory of the faithful. St Agnes, an early Roman martyr, still has an honourable mention in the Roman Canon of the Mass. The preacher might also wish to allude to the Church's devotion to the Blessed Virgin, to whom Keats delicately refers. The homiletic aim, however, is not to send people off to read Keats, but to point up from our lines the dignity of solitary piety and the stark stillness of God's mid-winter creation. That God is to be praised by the elements is the theme running right through the Canticle of Daniel – frost, cold and snow included. An allusion to it too might be incorporated.[4]

The plays of Bernard Shaw were produced from time to time in my old school (George Watson's, Edinburgh) under the direction of a gifted but eccentric master. I took part in two, *Caesar and Cleopatra* and *Saint Joan*. The author, that roguish old Irish agnostic, seems not only to have become interested in Joan's life, but to have succumbed to her sanctity as well. The play highlights the latter disarmingly, particularly in the Trial scene. I later produced that scene on its own for both junior and senior seminarians, who in their own way were spiritually affected too. One of Joan's speeches in that scene is of supreme merit, partly on account of Shaw's portrayal of the young woman's bravery and holiness, partly also because the prose is so vibrant as almost to become poetry at times. In fact it will respond to scansion in the central section. Here is part of it:

Bread has no sorrow for me, and water no affliction. But to shut me from the light of the sky and the sight of the fields and flowers; to chain my feet so that I can never ride again with the soldiers nor climb the hills; to make me breathe foul, damp darkness, and keep me from everything that brings me back to the love of God, when your wickedness and foolishness tempt me to hate him; all this is worse than the furnace in the Bible that was heated seven times; I could do without my warhorse, I could drag about in a skirt; I could let the banners and the trumpets and the knights and soldiers pass me and leave me behind as they leave the other women, if only I could hear the wind in the trees, the larks in the sunshine, the young lambs crying through the healthy frost, and the blessed, blessed church bells that send my angel voices floating to me on the wind. But without these things I cannot live, and by your wanting to take them away from me or from any human creature, I know that your counsel is of the devil and that mine is of God.[5]

Out of the richness of that passage there emerge: youthful courage in the face of dire peril; a moving act of personal faith; a graphic appreciation of the simple delights of nature; and an eloquent outburst against hypocrisy and political manipulation. Boyle's words recur: 'Representation is the moral reality of Redemption projected into the secular realm of pleasure.' First written for the entertainment of West End audiences, the play has values and lessons far deeper than the superficial requirements of the commercial theatre. The lines beginning 'I could do without my warhorse' could be incorporated verbatim into a homily of an appropriate theme, provided the standard of delivery was high.

In huge contrast I choose now a work by Francis Thompson, who died a century ago comparatively young. He seemed to be a failure. Judged to have no vocation to the Catholic priesthood, he subsequently abandoned medical studies, and left home to spend three years on the streets of London – destitute and opium-addicted. Though rescued by Alice and Wilfred Meynell, who oversaw the publication of his poems, he died from tuberculosis in 1907. His work has a mystic quality, not least his fine *The Hound of Heaven*, a powerful fantasy about the pursuit of the soul by Christ – 'this tremendous lover'. Autobiographical in many ways, the piece has wide relevance for any individual soul troubled by guilt or fear or scruples. On material of this kind Boyle said: 'We enjoy not the thing imitated, but the imitation. It is a terrible sight, but it is so beautifully painted, a terrible story, but so truthfully, so beautifully truthfully told.'[6]

The fearful soul's efforts to escape the Lord's pursuit finds dramatic expression in the opening lines which establish the mood to follow:

> I fled Him down the nights and down the days;
> I fled Him down the arches of the years;
> I fled Him down the labyrinthine ways
> Of my own mind; and in the mist of tears
> I hid from Him, and under running laughter.

The poet's realization that the chase is almost up elicits lines of considerable and effective pathos, thus:

> Yea, faileth now even the dream
> The dreamer, and the lute the lutanist;
> Even the linked fantasies, in whose blossomy twist
> I swung the earth a trinket at my wrist,
> Are yielding; cords of all too weak account
> For earth with heavy griefs so overplussed.
> Ah! is Thy love indeed
> A weed, albeit an amaranthine weed,
> Suffering no flowers except its own to mount?

Ah! Must –
Designer infinite! –
Ah! must Thou char the wood ere Thou canst limn with it?

Granted that there is a Victorian floridity of style in those lines, there is also an engaging momentum, and I know personally about the impact of the last two upon a dear relative whose life had been hard, for after her death there fell out of her Bible a scrap of paper, the same words written on it.

The long poem's conclusion is more familiar and much loved:

Halts by me that footfall:
Is my gloom, after all,
Shade of His hand outstretched caressingly?
'Ah, fondest, blindest, weakest,
I am He whom thou seekest!
Thou dravest love from thee, who dravest Me.'[7]

Listeners to a homily containing those words would not need to be drug-addicts or drop-outs. The moral is surely universal.

Thompson's approach seems to find analogous support from a modern thinker, Frederick Buechner, when he writes of another:

Let him tell them the truth ... Let him use words, but, in addition to using them to explain, expound, exhort, let him use them to evoke, to set us dreaming as well as thinking, to use words as at their most prophetic and truthful, as the prophets used them to stir in us memories and longings and intuitions that we starve for without knowing that we starve. Let him use words which do not only give answers to the questions that we ask or ought to ask, but which help us to hear the questions that we do not have words for asking, and to hear the silence that those questions rise out of and the silence that is the answer to those questions. Drawing on nothing fancier than the poetry of his own life, let him use words and images that help make the surface of our lives transparent to the truth that lies deep within them, which is the wordless truth of who we are and who God is and the gospel of our meeting.[8]

The phrase 'drawing on the poetry of his own life' is singularly apt for Thompson with his sensitive and imaginative spirit, but our paragraph's opening words, 'Let him tell them the truth' is apt too as we recall yet again the Boylian words: 'Literature seeks to tell the truth'.

My fourth example of a passage that has typically influenced my love affair with literature and with homiletics comes from Charles Dickens. Boyle quotes Chesterton when discussing 'the truth that secular literature can reveal to us through the pleasure of sharing', adding that:

Chesterton has said exactly what needs to be said in this connection about Dickens, far better than I could say it: 'The art of Dickens was the most exquisite of arts: it was the art of enjoying everybody ... I do not for a moment maintain that he enjoyed everybody in his daily life. But he enjoyed everybody in his books, and everybody has enjoyed everybody in those books even till today.'

Boyle is delighted to find that Chesterton 'recognizes the universality of the work of literature, and its call to all of us to share in it, as the route by which the secular leads to the sacred'.[9]

There is a splendid microcosm of the quirkiness of the

human condition in this extract from *Martin Chuzzlewit*,
the more unnerving the more we may refuse to recognize
anything of ourselves within it! The scene is a family
gathering:

> Then there were Anthony Chuzzlewit, and his son Jonas: the
> face of the old man so sharpened by the wariness and
> cunning of his life, that it seemed to cut him a passage
> through the crowded room, as he edged away behind the
> remotest chairs; while the son had so well profited by the
> precept and example of the father, that he looked a year or
> two the elder of the twain, as they stood winking their red
> eyes, side by side, and whispering to each other softly. Then
> there was the widow of a deceased brother of Mr Martin
> Chuzzlewit, who being almost supernaturally disagreeable,
> and having a dreary face, and a bony figure, and a
> masculine voice, was, in right of these qualities, what is
> commonly called a strong-minded woman; and who, if she
> could, would have established her claim to the title, and
> have shown herself, mentally speaking, a perfect Samson,
> by shutting up her brother-in-law in a private mad-house,
> until he proved his complete sanity by loving her very
> much. Beside her sat her spinster daughters, three in
> number, and of gentlemanly deportment, who had so
> mortified themselves with tight stays, that their tempers
> were reduced to something less than their waists, and sharp
> lacing was expressed in their very noses.[10]

Even in that account of such a ghastly collection of
relatives we can sense Dickens' humour being at once
incisive and curiously sympathetic. This must be due to
his conviction that human beings of their very nature
really matter. Boyle again: 'Enjoying everybody without
the belief that they matter would be the act of a Don Juan,
who in the end condemns himself to the same eternal
meaninglessness that he assumes in his victims.'[11]

My fifth 'influence' goes back at least forty years, since the days in the 1960s when I took fifth- and sixth-year boys in Blairs College (Junior Seminary, Aberdeen) for English. Gerard Manley Hopkins became, and has remained, one of my favourite poets for several reasons, of which these are three: first, his vigorous, innovative mastery of prosody; secondly, his love of beauty in man and in nature (influenced in part by Keats, we are told); and thirdly, what the *Oxford Book of English Literature* has called 'his search for a unifying sacramental view of creation' (the major influence here, scholars say, being the thirteenth-century Franciscan polymath, John Duns Scotus).[12] The fact that the present writer is a Catholic priest and a 'convert' gives me a fellow feeling, a kind of spiritual identity, with the distinguished Jesuit.

Hopkins' poetic output was in abeyance for years since he found versifying incompatible with the exigencies of religious life. His work, a small corpus, won little recognition for some years after his death in 1889, until it was championed and promoted by his friend Robert Bridges.

The following poem, the sonnet *The Caged Skylark*, encompasses within its fourteen lines anger over the captivity of a lovely wild bird, a comparison of the creature's lot with that of a man entrapped in his physical body (possibly reflecting Plato's similar thoughts in the *Gorgias*, 493A, the *soma sema* section), and a serene rumination about 'the resurrection of the body' at the end of time:

As a dare-gale skylark scanted in a dull cage
Man's mounting spirit in his bone-house, mean house,
    dwells –
That bird remembering his free fells;

This in drudgery, day-labouring-out life's age.
Though aloft on turf or perch or poor low stage,
Both sing sometimes the sweetest, sweetest spells,
Yet both droop deadly sometimes in their cells
Or wring their barriers in bursts of fear or rage.
Not that the sweet-fowl, song-fowl, needs no rest –
Why, hear him, hear him babble and drop down to his
     nest,
But his own nest, wild nest, no prison.
Man's spirit will be flesh-bound when found at best,
But uncumbered: meadow-down is not distressed
For a rainbow footing it nor he for his bones risen.[13]

The last three lines bring upon me the kind of pain experienced by many when faced with artistic perfection in music, art, or literature. Hopkins here 'seeks to tell the truth' by creating two lovely images which illuminate the profession of faith in 'We look for the resurrection of the dead'. In which connection two other authors, St Cyril of Jerusalem[14] and C. S. Lewis,[15] both writing in flights of imagination, run parallel with Hopkins' thought. The former:

> He that year by year raises up the corn which we sow, when it is dead, shall He find difficulty in raising us up, for whose sakes He was raised Himself? Thou seest how the trees have stood now for so many months fruitless and leafless, but when the winter is passed they revive in all their parts as it were from the dead. Shall we then not much rather, yea and much more easily, live again?

And C. S. Lewis:

> Then the new earth and sky, the same yet not the same as these, will rise in us as we have risen in Christ. And once

again, after who knows what aeons of the silence and the dark, the birds will sing out and the waters flow, and lights and shadows move across the hills and the faces of our friends laugh upon us with amazed recognition. Guesses, of course, only guesses. If they are not true, something better will be. For we know that we shall be made like Him, for we shall see Him as He is.

'Influences' thus far have moved from the child-saint Agnes to middle-aged Hopkins via the nonagenarian Shaw. The remaining two are concerned with death in positive vein. The first comes from the autobiography of Lord Norwich (Duff Cooper) and is reflectively optimistic:

> I have never felt that the contemplation of the past with the knowledge that it cannot come again, need be a source of sorrow ... Life has been good to me and I am grateful. My delight in it is as keen as ever and I will thankfully accept as many more years as may be granted ... I shall not be too distressed when the summons comes to go away. Autumn has always been my favourite season, and evening has been for me the pleasantest time of day. I love the sunlight but I cannot fear the coming of the dark.[16]

I wonder if he had Browning's *Prospice* in mind when he wrote those words. In any event, the pastoral need to reassure people, Christian or not, when death is in prospect can superimpose a passage such as Cooper's upon the affirming and consoling truths of the gospels, and be a practical aid in preaching. 'Literature,' declares Boyle, 'I think, shows us in words the truth about life.' Clearly it has, *mutatis mutandis*, something profitable to say about death too.

Whereas the Cooper excerpt has been a comparatively recent 'influence', the final piece has been part of my literary and spiritual armoury for twenty-five years. It is an anonymous poem of the seventeenth century, and purports to be a dialogue between one of the robbers ('the good thief') being crucified beside Christ, and a curious but sceptical interlocutor. It runs:

> Say bold but blessed thief
> That in a trice
> Slipped into paradise,
> And in plain day
> Stol'st heaven away,
> What trick couldst thou invent
> To compass thy intent?
> What arms?
> What charms?
> 'Love and belief.'
>
> Say bold but blessed thief,
> How couldst thou read
> A crown upon that head?
> What text, what gloss,
> A kingdom on a cross?
> How couldst thou come to spy
> God in a man to die?
> What light?
> What sight?
> 'The sight of grief –
>
> I sight to God his pain;
> And by that sight
> I saw the light;
> Thus did my grief
> Beget relief.
> And take this rule from me,
> Pity thou him, he'll pity thee.

Use this,
Ne'er miss,
Heaven may be stol'n again.'[17]

The poem itself is finely crafted, the inquiries being not merely inquisitive but doubtful about this ruffian's motivation. The tenderness of the replies reflects admirably the tone of the verses in St Luke's Gospel that record the incident.[18] To the other thief, railing against Christ, the first says: '"Do you not fear God, since you are under the same sentence of condemnation? And we indeed justly; for we are receiving the due reward of our deeds, but this man has done nothing wrong." And he said: "Jesus, remember me when you come into your kingdom." And Jesus said to him, "Truly, I say to you, today you will be with me in Paradise."' This brief account (given only in St Luke) has sometimes been called 'the gospel within the Gospel'.

Mgr Ronald Knox, stressing the beauty of accepting God's pardon at the eleventh hour, speaks of the thief 'who, on the impulse of the moment, yielded to the pursuit of those nailed feet, the beckoning of those motionless hands'.[19] 'It is not too late,' he adds, 'to devote what remains of life, though it be but the spent ashes of a life, to all outward seeming, in service of God's vineyard.' One particular sculpture depicting this scene has moved me greatly over sixty years. It is by Fr Marie Bernard of the Abbaye Grande Trappe, Orne, and taken together with our Bible-based poem, seems to justify a sentence encountered recently: 'If the preaching of the word of God is to flourish, then we need poets and artists, singers and musicians who keep alive that intuition of our ultimate destiny.'[20] Add to that Boyle's contention that: 'the Christian faith ... is the faith that Christ's redeeming work continues, bringing within the ever newly redrawn boundaries of God's kingdom his ever newly adopted children.' He continues:

> Read as showing Christ in the moment in which they mark themselves off from their origin in God, secular scriptures become the limit case of sacred scripture, the word of God no longer as an address to us – as God's reply to our prayer – but as the inarticulate groanings of the Spirit within us – as our prayer itself.[21]

Three poetry selections and three prose – indicative, it is hoped, of three things in order of significance: a catholicity of taste in the author of this discourse, a hint of the enormous range available to the homilist from literary sources, and my continuing indebtedness to Professor Boyle, and to his axiom:

> Secular literature ... takes a non-purposive enjoyment in the being of things which, to the extent that it approaches the state of pure authorless writtenness – for it can never actually attain that state – is capable of foreshadowing a revelation of Being and of the fundamental – pre-original – modification of Being by ethical obligation.[22]

Fr Daniel O'Leary, a priest of the Leeds diocese and a regular contributor to *The Tablet* writes in the issue of 21 July 2007 in an article entitled *Lost but for words*, in Boylian style:

> Jesus actually was, and is, in his utter humanity, the mother tongue of God. The Gospels speak of Christ as 'the Word' – the Word of Love. Like this Word, then, all words – especially those of hierarchy, of liturgy, of teaching and preaching – are small incarnations of Being that is Love. In

Words for It, Julia Cameron captures the yearnings of both mother and lover for bringing words to life:

> I wish I could take language and fold it like cool, moist
> rags.
> I would lay words on your forehead. I would wrap
> words on your wrist.
> 'There, there,' my words would say – or something
> even better.
> I would ask them to murmur, 'Hush' and 'Shh, shh, it's
> all right.'
> I would ask them to hold you all night.
> I wish I could take language and daub and soothe and
> cool
> Where fever blisters and burns, where fever turns
> yourself against you.
> I wish I could take language and heal the words that
> were the wounds
> You have no name for.[23]

Some of the roots from which my preaching ministry has grown have been indicated. Like most roots, however, prudent and assiduous watering has had to continue over the years. The extent to which such growth has occurred will be put to the test in the next chapter, the thrust of which will be concerned with the 'praxis' of preaching. It will not ignore areas of shortcoming, but hopes to show how the use of literature within homilies, if applied intelligently and prudently, may indeed be a practical aid to their effectiveness.

Notes

1. Southey, R., *The Doctor*, Vol. I (Longman, Rees, Orme, Brown, Green and Longman, London, 1834), p. 172.

2. Boyle, pp. 133–4.
3. *The English Parnassus*, p. 499.
4. Roman Canon (Eucharistic Prayer I), Ch. III, v. 57ff.
5. *Saint Joan*, scene 6, in G. B. Shaw, *The Complete Plays of George Bernard Shaw* (Odham's Press Ltd., London, 1934), 1000.
6. Boyle, p. 130.
7. *Poetry of the English Speaking World*, ed. R. Aldington (Heinemann, London, 1947), pp. 825–9.
8. Buechner, F., *Telling the Truth* (Harper Collins, London, 1977), pp. 23–4.
9. Boyle, p. 131.
10. Dickens, C., *Martin Chuzzlewit*, (Nelson Classics, Edinburgh 1964), chapter 4.
11. Boyle, p. 132.
12. *Oxford Book of English Literature*, 5th edition (Oxford University Press, Oxford, 1989), p. 473.
13. *Poems of Gerard Manley Hopkins*, p. 75.
14. St Cyril of Jerusalem, *Procatechesis Lecture III*, 'Of the Resurrection'.
15. Lewis, C. S., *Letters to Malcolm* (Geoffrey Bles, London, 1964), p. 158.
16. Quoted in D. Worlock, *Take One at Bedtime* (Sheed and Ward, London, 1962), p. 67.
17. 'The Thief', in *Christian Poetry Collection*, ed. M. Bachelor (Lion Books, Oxford, 1995), p. 525.
18. Luke 23:40–43.
19. Knox, R. A., *Pastoral Sermons* (Burns Oates, London, 1959), p. 144.
20. Radcliffe, T., *Grace and Task of Preaching*, p. 123.
21. Boyle, pp. 144–5.
22. Boyle, p. 138.
23. O'Leary, D., in *The Tablet* (21 July 2007), p. 15.

Chapter 4

Preaching as Praxis

Tolle, lege! Tolle, lege!
(St Augustine, *Confessions*, VIII, 12)

The ministry of preaching derives from Christ's command to his disciples: 'Go ye, therefore, and teach all nations ... teaching them to observe all things whatsoever I have commanded you; and lo, I am with you always, even to the end of the world' (Mt 28:19–20).

Having already examined (with Boyle and Radcliffe) what is meant by 'literature', we must turn directly to the matter of preaching. The preaching commissioned by Our Lord has necessarily become an important part of the teaching; and discipleship, for Peter and the other apostles in their time, is a matter of learning, or at least a willingness to learn, how best to proclaim the Gospel.

Among early writings on the subject is the following from the second-century martyr, St Justin:

On Sunday there is an assembly of all who live in towns or in the country, and the memoirs of the apostles or the writings of the prophets are read for as long as time allows. Then the reading is brought to an end, and the president delivers an address, in which he admonishes and encourages us to imitate in our own lives the beautiful lessons we have heard read.[1]

It is salutary for a Catholic priest to be clear about the
place of preaching in the liturgy from an early date, for a
latent conviction persists that the proclamation of the
word is primarily the province of the Reformed
traditions. The late Fr John O'Donnell of the Pontifical
Gregorian University in Rome wrote an article called
'Ministers of the Word' for the *Scots College Magazine*
(2006 edition), and introduced it thus:

> I think that most of us, when we reflect on our vocation to
> the priesthood, naturally tend to focus on our role as
> sacramental ministers. And we find our place most easily at
> the Lord's table where we preside at the Eucharist. At the
> same time it seems to me ever more urgent to recall and to
> foster our vocation as ministers of God's Word. As Vatican
> II's decree on priesthood noted: 'The people of God finds its
> unity first of all through the Word of the living God which
> is quite properly sought from the lips of priests.'

Later in the article the author states:

> I am convinced that Catholics today have a hunger for God's
> Word. They come to Sunday Mass with a desire for life, a
> longing for spiritual nourishment. Unfortunately too often
> they receive too little to give them sustenance on their
> journey. Catholics often complain bitterly about the quality
> of preaching in their local parishes.[2]

Fr Timothy Radcliffe ruminates:

> Boring and ineffectual preaching has been a problem from
> the very beginning. Indeed Webster's Dictionary defines to
> preach as 'to give moral or religious advice, especially in a
> tiresome manner' ... I console myself by remembering that
> St Paul droned on at such length that Eutyches fell asleep
> and dropped to his death ... When St Caesarius of Arles

preached, his sermons were so tedious that the doors had to be locked to stop the people from fleeing![3]

The American Jesuit, Fr Walter J. Burghardt is even more trenchant:

> ... the long-suffering laity are intolerant of the trivia we dish out, the constipation of thought amid a diarrhoea of words, are surprised and scandalized by a dismal style and a vapid vocabulary unworthy of the word we claim to proclaim, and are puzzled by our ability to declaim about the divine without a shred of feeling or emotion.[4]

Chaucer in his day inveighed against inferior preachers and preachments. Let one example suffice, this boast of the Pardoner:

> 'My lords,' he said, 'in churches where I preach
> I cultivate a haughty kind of speech
> And ring it out as roundly as a bell;
> I've got it all by heart, this tale I tell.
> I have a text, it always is the same
> And always has been, since I learned the game,
> Old as the hills and fresher than the grass,
> *Radix malorum est cupiditas.*'[5]
> ('The root of evil is greed.')

Germane to our study are these points: first, that preaching has a vital part to fulfil within public liturgies, and secondly, that the chief purpose of the homily is to provide spiritual nourishment. May it never be said of our efforts that 'the hungry sheep look up, and are not fed'.[6]

Deacon Duncan MacPherson, in a robust paper entitled *Homiletics and Lection* declares:

The aim of proclamation in the Ministry of Word is to involve the participants in what is heard and to call forth the response of the hearer to the disclosure of God's seeking love. Anyone who is engaged in proclaiming or preaching needs first to have the aim of communicating this vision of life-transforming good news.[7]

The style of homiletics has inevitably changed over the centuries. So also has sermon length (circuitous masters like St Augustine or St John Chrysostom would preach for up to two hours!). The aim, however, has been constant to interpret Scripture for God's people in a manner that is orthodox, strong, and pastorally upbuilding.

Within the Ordination rite for priests and deacons the bishop says to the candidates:

> You must apply your energies to the duty of teaching in the name of Christ, the chief Teacher. Share with all mankind the word of God you have received with joy. Meditate on the law of God, believe what you read, teach what you believe, and put into practice what you teach.

A homily ought primarily to be an elucidation, not a lecture, a proclamation, not a performance. All the same, the doughty St Augustine would have qualified that last assertion, as Burghardt points out:

> He encouraged reactions from his audience, found applause stimulating, provocative: 'What is there to cheer about? We are still battling with the problem and you have already started to cheer!' He saw the sermon as not only education but entertainment: 'You must not believe, brothers and sisters, that the Lord intended us to be entirely without theatrical spectacles of some kind. If there were none here, would you have come together in this place?'[8]

Early on, the Church took a dim view about the skills of rhetoric, despite their esteem by the Greeks and Romans, and though St Paul himself had been trained in them. Tertullian demanded to know, however: 'What has Athens to do with Jerusalem?'[9] And in our time, eloquence as an art must be admired, but even a masterly display from a preacher courts shallowness and self-indulgence if the gospel message is subject to it alone. A down-to-earth servitor at Edinburgh University once remarked to students queuing up to get into the New North Kirk: 'Och, you just go there to have Dr Sclater tickle your ears!'

On reflecting on the responsibility of his task and conscious of his unworthiness, the preacher may be tempted to shy away from it. Seen, however, as an integral part of his ministry, as something bound up with his lifetime's apostolate, preaching the Gospel will become not a liturgical chore but an exciting pastoral opportunity. The more it is seen as working for the Lord within a missionary church, the more fruitful and humble his task will be. He is, after all, merely God's instrument.

Staying briefly with the word 'instrument', we find John Donne, that erratic genius, picturing himself late in life and making ready to join the sainted musicians in heaven:

> Since I am coming to that holy room,
> Where, with thy choir of saints for evermore,
> I shall be made thy music; as I come
> I tune the instrument here at the door,
> And what I must do then, think here before.[10]

The clergy, and indeed all God's people, may helpfully be regarded as a large orchestral force, the Almighty being the musical director. We tune *our* instruments, raise *our* voices in ongoing praise of the Saviour. Our earthly lives may be but an overture, a prelude until the curtain rises on the life to come. God has, let us say, provided us with the score. It is up to us assiduously to practise our scales prayerfully day by day, with something of the anticipation John Donne has outlined in his verses. To have a true effect, the notes being played must be in accord with the wishes of the musical director, whose purposes require the co-operation of all from the least to the greatest, from the piccolo, as it were, to the double-bass.

As breath is to the body, prayer is to the soul. It is accordingly of capital importance that prayer should accompany the planning of a homily. St Augustine leaves us in no doubt: 'He is a vain preacher of the word of God without, who is not a hearer within.'[11] Or again: 'Whether you are at this very moment about to preach to a congregation, or to give a talk to any kind of group, you should pray that God may put good words into your mouth.'[12]

How much room is there in homiletics for variety of approach and presentation? Considerable room, for we are dealing usually from week to week with a wide range of readings and of individual clergymen expounding them. Rigid precepts cannot apply, though preachers should prepare and deliver their message in accordance with Church teaching and practice.

For those of us ordained to the priesthood prior to the Second Vatican Council the sermon had become the Cinderella of the liturgy. The Conciliar reforms were generally welcome, and the first of all the documents to be published was *Sacrosanctum Concilium* (4 December

1963), dealing with the shape and structure of the Mass. Much stress was laid upon the function of the 'liturgy of the word', and upon the inclusion of a homily within it after the proclamation of the Gospel, particularly on Sundays and major festivals. There would be no further syllabuses of sermon topics provided annually by diocesan bishops. A lectionary was approved for use in every parish of the Roman rite. Hence far more Scripture than previously was available for use throughout the year – a two-year cycle of readings for weekdays and a three-year cycle for Sundays. The riches of Scripture were thus made far more accessible to churchgoers. In addition, preachers had the opportunity to study, interpret and deliver a far wider range of readings and homilies for the benefit of their flocks and of themselves.

Here are the unambiguous words of the *General Instruction of the Roman Missal* (1974):

> When the scriptures are read in the church, God himself speaks to his people, and it is Christ present in his word who proclaims the gospel ... In the Biblical readings God's word is addressed to all men and women of every era and is understandable in itself, but a homily, as a living explanation of the word, increases its effectiveness and is an integral part of the service (9).

While Sunday homilies are of obligation, weekday sermonettes are a desirable option. The liturgical context is what differentiates a homily from a sermon, the latter being as a rule a 'free-standing' preachment that develops a text or theme not rooted in the prescribed readings or texts of the day.

Careful control of literary input is essential, for if it is abused or overused its advantages will be quite negated.

Professor Boyle, with whom I had a recent conversation, told me that *his* zeal about the use of literature in preaching was kindled by the Dominican scholar Kenelm Foster, an authority on St Thomas Aquinas and on Dante, allusions to and quotations from whose poetry were skilfully but sparingly worked into his homiletic material. Faithfulness to the pastoral, missiological purposes of preaching has to come first. In a word, the end of all preaching is to bring one's parish and oneself into a closer relationship with God through the proclamation of the good news.

Here is an excerpt from the *Diatesseron* of St Ephraim (4th century) dealing with the impact of the word of God and its beauty. I quote it since it is encouragingly consonant with my personal convictions:

> Lord, who can grasp the wealth of just one of your words? What we understand is much less than what we leave behind, like thirsty people who drink from a fountain. For your word, Lord, has many shades of meaning, just as those who study it have many different points of view. The Lord has coloured his words with many hues, so that each person who studies it can see in it what he loves.

My task is to see how written words – what Boyle calls 'secular scriptures'[13] – can be set alongside Scripture in preaching for purposes of illustration and stimulus. The words of poets will be referred to often, whilst we realize how poetical parts of the Bible itself are. There is a century-old collection of sayings by the then professor of Hebrew in Edinburgh's New College, John Duncan. From it comes this scholarly assertion:

There is scarcely a species of literature not represented in it [the Bible]. There is no order of magnificence, in poetry for example, which we do not find in Isaiah. He is sublimely tender, yet majestically stormy . . . There's a wild rugged and abrupt sternness in Ezekiel. He stands midway between the majestic sublimity of Isaiah and the elegiacs of Jeremiah . . . The poetry of the sublime rises to its very highest level in Scripture, because we have the sublimity of form added to the sublimity of the theme . . . And what is there finer in all secular literature, as poetry alone, than the song of the angels: 'Glory to God in the highest, on earth peace, goodwill to men'?[14]

Bearing in mind the points made in Chapter One by Timothy Radcliffe and Nicholas Boyle, we may rejoice over the insights they have brought concerning the 'sacred and secular scripture' proposition which is our overriding concern. The whole issue is less of a problem than a challenge requiring sensitive handling. As for Kenelm Foster, OP, so for us, common sense and discretion will give guidance.

Literature finds a happy alliance with Scripture in three main ways: first, when the words of an author, succinctly or memorably written, themselves make a direct homiletic impact; secondly, when such quotations serve to point up and illumine the gospel message; and thirdly, where an author's genius may lighten or brighten the lives of a congregation in particular circumstances of joy or sorrow. It has already been argued (in Chapter One) that, while Christian writers are likely to be most frequently quoted, those of other religions or none may be used. It was interesting to discover from Ronald Blythe's Introduction to George Herbert's *The Country Parson* how the latter had a predilection for aphorisms and proverbs in his preaching. Indeed, in the section entitled *The Parson Preaching*, Herbert declares: 'Sometimes he [the preacher] tells them stories, and sayings of others, according as his text invites him; for them also men heed, and remember better than exhortations.'[15] A forward hint, here, of 'sacred and secular scriptures'?

Herbert himself, Hopkins and T. S. Eliot stand out among many to have used the Bible for their inspiration. Ezra Pound (*il miglior fabbro*) is said to have teased Eliot for preferring Moses to the Muses! A much earlier poet, Thomas Traherne, may be suggesting that a guide, literary or exegetical, might be helpful to a timorous or unaided reader or hearer of the Bible. In his lines *On the Bible* he writes:

> It is a sign thou wantest sound intelligence
> If that thou think thyself to understand the sense;
> Be not deceived thou then on it in vain mayst gaze;
> The way is intricate that leads into a maze.[16]

Probably with Scripture in mind, the former bishop of Durham, Michael Turnbull, commented morosely: 'preaching may at times be likened to playing squash against a haystack, there being neither comeback, resonance, or anticipation!'[17]

Literary sources other than those within the Christian tradition present no problem. Take two of English poetry's greatest heritages, the Bible and the Classics. From the latter, Virgil's fourth or 'Messianic' Eclogue, written in 40 BC, anticipated the birth of a child who would bring back the Golden Age. In the Middle Ages this was regarded as a prophecy of the birth of Christ, largely because the piece contains imagery strongly reminiscent of Scripture. The

connection is now known to be erroneous, but clearly the
pagan poet was not felt to be beyond the pale. In prose too
the ground is rich for a homiletic forager to find lines or
phrases from great thinkers like Plato and Aristotle on the
Greek side, and even Cicero (in milder works such as his
De Amicitia or *Hortensius*, which strongly influenced St
Augustine) on the Roman. Why fix boundaries upon
literary eras when style and wisdom were in masterly
hands? Let us further suppose that a Catholic priest is due
to preach on the festival of the Immaculate Conception and
that he is of a literary bent. He could do no better than refer
to Wordsworth, that avowed pantheist, who penned the
following couplet:

> Woman, above all women glorified,
> Our tainted nature's solitary boast.[18]

Quotations either obscure or mumbled are
unacceptable, especially where poetry or verse-drama is
involved. A measure of training would ideally be required
for the latter. Inadequate projection (even with a
microphone) or any other form of carelessness will not
do. Ruth Gledhill, in her Foreword to the *Times Book of
Best Sermons*, offers salutary counsel:

> To read aloud – even for ten minutes a day – is to instil
> cadence and rhythm, style and sonority into the memory's
> ear. Whether Beatrix Potter or Edward Lear, Shakespeare's
> sonnets or Dickens or Lewis Carroll or the five-star hot-shot
> Prefaces to the 1611 *Authorized Version of the Bible*: any
> sparkling poetry or prose can help to kindle a scintillating
> sermon. So too will masterly sermons of the past ... And of
> course, a quick dip into the treatises by Cicero or Quintilian
> will crisp even the most limp sermon style.[19]

By now, it is hoped, a clearer way forward is emerging, and it can be seen how the 'sacred and secular scriptures' of the previous chapter deserve appropriate and intelligent proclamation. St Augustine asks his congregation in one of his sermons:

> What do I desire? Why do I speak? Why do I sit here? Why do I live, if not for this reason, that together we might live in Christ? This is my desire, this my honour, my glory, my joy, my possession. But if you will not listen to me, and still I am not silent, I shall redeem my own soul. But I do not want to be saved without you.[20]

Augustine's own salvation and that of his hearers are intimately connected. No less in our own day, the spiritual bond between preacher and people should be alive and productive. In his recent book, *Go, Tell Them*,[21] Fr Robert Hendrie quotes an article by Peter Drilling from *Lonergan Workshop*:[22]

> While preaching's principal object is the Word of God, it is not the Word of God in its original context as the Word of God, which is the object of Biblical exegesis and interpretation in the way they are practised in the academy. The object of preaching is the Word of God addressing this congregation within this liturgy in order to lead to adoration, praise and thanksgiving at this time and to Christian living in the world as the congregation moves beyond this particular act of worship. This complication of preaching's object gives sermons their particular temporality – a sermon is remarkably 'ad hoc', almost like a daily newspaper.

While broadly agreeing with that, I would venture to suggest that an admixture of fine secular literature within a sermon may rescue it from the brashness and braggadocio of the tabloid publications and give it a whiff of timelessness.

Fr Daniel Francis, CSsR, has written a forceful essay,[23] entitled *The pulpit is a mountain*. Referring to preachers he writes,

> Our task is to accompany people up the mountain to get a better view of the realm of God in their lives, so that when they find themselves in the shadow of the valley of pain, confusion, death, or some other darkness, they may recognize that God is there as well. This is heaven on earth, the inbreaking of the Realm, God's grace actualized so that all may have life abundantly. The pulpit is a mountain. The preaching moment supplies the necessary experience of liminality, the 'between space' or threshold for the encounter with God.

Those words tie in neatly with what Nicholas Boyle (quoted in Chapter One) had to say about the legitimacy of using tragedy as a constituent part of 'secular scriptures'. Fr Francis goes on to quote the conclusion of Isaiah chapter 25:

> It will be said on that day, Lo, this is our God; we have waited for him, so that he might save us. This is the Lord for whom we have waited; let us be glad and rejoice in his salvation. For the hand of the Lord will rest on this mountain (25:6).

Parallel with Fr Francis' thinking are the following words from Pope John Paul II's Apostolic Exhortation, *Pastores Dabo Vobis*, issued in 1992:

> The priest is first of all a minister of God. He is consecrated and sent forth to proclaim the Good News of the Kingdom to all, calling every person to the obedience of faith, and

leading believers to an ever-increasing knowledge of and communion in the mystery of God, as revealed and communicated to us in Christ ... Only if he 'abides' in the word will the priest become a perfect disciple of the Lord ... The priest ought to be the first 'believer' in the word, while being fully aware that the words of his ministry are not 'his', but those of the One who sent him. He is not the master of the word, but its servant. He is not the sole possessor of the word; in its regard he is in debt to the People of God (26).

The Pope's words depend upon Matthew 28:19–20, the text which opened this chapter. Commenting on the same text with renewed optimism is an essay within the *Lectionary Commentary*[24] by Craig S. Keener:

We may wish to remember that in Matthew's day followers of Jesus remained an insignificantly small percentage of the Mediterranean world, and could embrace this command and promise only by great faith. Whatever our obstacles today – and they are many – the first generations of the Church managed to believe and spread their message in the face of greater hostility. Miraculously, they multiplied into the numbers of Christians today that the first generations could hardly have imagined.

My wish is to build upon the central importance of the Bible in preaching, and to examine, as Nicholas Boyle puts it:

... the extent to which secular, that is, non-biblical and non-sacred writing can be read, at times, with the advantage with which, at times, the Bible also can be read. The result, I hope, is the discovery of some new ways in which some of the greatest modern literature – and also some of the less great – can speak to us about the relation of the modern world to God, about God's hiddenness, and about his reconciliation of our world to himself through his Son and through his Son's mystical body, the church.[25]

The present challenge is to see to what extent, in the light of Professor Boyle's argumentation, it is possible to preach as well as to read 'non-biblical and non-sacred writing', at times, with the advantage with which, at times, the Bible can be preached. What has emerged from the first chapter is going to influence this study's further investigations, and will use as a kind of leitmotif the Boylian dictum: 'literature is language free from instrumental purpose, and it seeks to tell the truth'.

The last sentence's transparency may be set against the opaque thinking of R. S. Thomas in his poem, *Kneeling*:

> Prompt me, God;
> But not yet. When I speak,
> Though it be you who speak
> Through me, something is lost.
> The meaning is in the waiting.[26]

Enigmatic, certainly; yet the idea of God as the prompter and the clergyman as an actor has deep implications. And it takes a poem to express it.

The 'waiting' experience mentioned by Thomas can suddenly cease. It occasionally has for me, and doubtless for a myriad of other preachers; and a recent poem by the Irish Dominican, Fr Paul Murray, vividly depicts an instance where, for him, the 'waiting' is interrupted:

> The text opens like a river
> in full spate. Or, it's like a window
> opening with a sudden gust of wind.
> And it's as if an archangel

had entered the room. And everybody
has to stop what they're doing.
And the air *is a river of divine words* [my italics]
And all of a sudden you see
– and with a start –
that an archangel has entered,
and your heart is in your mouth.
And you feel you are drowning
in a river of divine words, and hear [my italics]
yourself saying, over and over,
'How can this be?'[27]

The words of Eli to Samuel (1 Samuel 3:9): 'Speak, Lord, for thy servant hears' may be a prerequisite for such incidents as those lines describe. Generally, however, whilst prayerfully listening for God's voice is paramount, being aware of the sound as well as the sense of words has its place too.

The material of the following chapter is wide-ranging, but depends upon the preceding one insofar as the practical side of this reflection is concerned. It will look at aspects of sermon preparation, of the value of the homilist's having built up a 'private treasure-trove' of literature, of his need for flexibility. The importance to him of the Arts as a whole will be stressed, and hymnology will briefly be considered before the power of certain key authors is discussed, including some Scots. Three anthologies are particularly recommended for the perusal of homilists, and the chapter ends with three authoritative 'slants', views about the very essence of preaching with which this writer concurs.

Notes

1. *The First Apology* of St Justin, Martyr, *In defence of the Christians*, ch. 66.
2. *Presbyterorum Ordinis*, no. 4.
3. Radcliffe, T., in *Grace and Task of Preaching*, p. 108.
4. Burghardt, W. J., *Preaching, the art and craft* (Paulist Press, New York, 1987), p. 84.
5. Chaucer, *The Canterbury Tales: The Prologue to the Pardoner's Tale*, lines 43–8.
6. Milton, J. *Lycidas*, line 123.
7. MacPherson, D., *Homiletics and Lection* (Maryvale Institute, Birmingham, 2005), p. 18.
8. Burghardt, *Preaching*, p. 82.
9. Tertullian, *De Praescriptione*, PL2, column 20.
10. 'Hymn to God in my Sickness', in *John Donne: Complete Poetry and Selected Prose*, ed. J. Hayward (Nonesuch Press, London, 1942), p. 320.
11. St Augustine, *Sermons*, 179,1.
12. Ibid., *De Doctrina Christiana*, IV, 30, 63.
13. Cf. Chapter 1, *passim*.
14. Knight, W. A., *Colloquia Peripatetica: Being Notes of Conversations with John Duncan LL.D.* (David Douglas, Edinburgh, 1879), p. 127.
15. Herbert, G., *The Country Parson,* ed. R. Blythe (Canterbury Press, Norwich, 2003), p. 15.
16. *Chapters Into Verse: A Selection of Poetry in English Inspired by the Bible from Genesis Through Revelation*, ed. R. Atwan and L. Wieder (Oxford University Press, Oxford, 2000), p. 5.
17. Foreword to *The Times Book of Best Sermons*, ed. R. Gledhill (Cassell, London, 1998).
18. Wordsworth, W., *Ecclesiastical Sonnets*, Part II, no. 25.
19. *The Fifth Times Book of Best Sermons*, (Cassell, London, 1999), p. xiv.
20. St Augustine, *Sermons,* 17, 2.
21. Hendrie, R., *Go, Tell Them*, p. 237.
22. *Lonergan Workshop* Vol. 7 (Scholars Press, Atlanta, Georgia, 1988), pp. 99ff.
23. Heille, G., *Theology of Preaching: Essays on Vision and Mission in the Pulpit* (Melisande, London, 2001), p. 89.
24. Kenner, C. S., 'Matthew 28:16-20', in *Lectionary Commentary: Theological Exegesis for Sunday's Texts*, iii, ed.

R. E. Van Harn (Eerdmans Publishing Co., Grand Rapids, Michigan, 2001), 161.

25. Boyle, p. 113.
26. Thomas, *Collected Poems*, p. 199.
27. *Sacred Space*, p. 79.

Chapter 5

A Literary Learning Curve

Atque inter silvas Academi quaerere verum
('And to seek the truth amid the groves of Academus')[1]

Over the years my views and practices as a homilist have developed and matured. My desire to proclaim the Gospel has always been passionate, wedded to the conviction that for some proclaimers literature and the Bible, far from being incompatible with one another, can be brought into homiletic harmony without detriment to their respective values. Where this combination can be achieved between 'sacred' and 'secular' scripture (as I am now used to calling them), the latter may bestow upon the former a new vitality and interest. Hearers of the Word might come in this way to fresh appreciations and exciting insights, in terms both of relevance and revelation in their lives.

I am the happy inheritor of a love of words bequeathed to me by my parents. At my school in Edinburgh attention was concentrated on writers of the 18th and 19th centuries and on Shakespeare. We all rebelled at being forced to read set novels, but, when it came to poetry, I gladly learned pieces off by heart, and wonder whether the ceasing of this practice in schools today is wise. Many older folk find that passages from Shakespeare or the great lyric poets visit the memory like the voices of old friends.

Keats' *Ode to Autumn* awakened my zeal, and his *The Eve of St Agnes* too (see Ch. 3). As for prose works, Dickens (rather than Scott) and Jane Austen (rather than George Eliot) delighted me.

Coming to the study of Latin and Greek, I was taught to understand, little by little, something of the beauty of Virgil and Horace, and of Homer. The Greek tragedians were a source of enjoyment later, but what a trial it was to plough through the then newly-published edition of *Agamemnon* by Professor Fraenkel of Oxford, with its dauntingly erudite commentary. Aeschylus became more attractive later, when I took part in a production of the same play (in Greek) in the Arts Theatre, Cambridge.

Both at school and University I found myself among singularly gifted fellow-students. My indebtedness to my old Classics teacher is enormous, his strong desire being that we should aim for excellence.

Two circumstances of my youth led me Biblewards. First came my mother's conversion to Catholicism when I was ten; secondly, the daily school assemblies at George Watson's, led by the then headmaster Ian Graham Andrew, whose reading of Scripture, especially the Psalms, was compelling. To my Presbyterian origins I owe much, and to a family circle that at one time included several ministers. Still, to have escaped from the *longueur* (as it seemed) of kirk sermons was a boon. Interminable preachments have this in common with the Loch Ness monster, for each has a beginning, then a middle, and a middle, and a middle, and the tail-end is a long time a-coming! One recalls the anecdote about the great Thomas Chalmers (leader of the Church of Scotland

Disruption in 1843), who is said to have told a long-winded student to cut out half his sermon, and it didn't matter *which* half!

Students have occasionally asked me (in seminary or at the Catholic chaplaincy in Aberdeen) how to go about preparing a homily. I have had little new to offer them. The snap-answer is 'leave nothing to chance', but a more considered reply would insist that preparation, remote and proximate, must have a dual basis: total conviction about the sacredness of proclaiming the word of God, and avoidance of any form of self-indulgence. Whereupon it might be objected: 'What about all those literary references you keep bringing in?' To which the response would have to be that their only justification is their enhancement of the gospel message in a manner that is fresh – as if varnish were to be applied to a wonderful painting. Preachers should not start off by thinking: what can I purloin from reputable authors around which a scripture-based homily may be framed? No. The word of God, and it alone, is paramount. We have seen, however (Ch. 1), how what Nicholas Boyle describes as 'secular' scripture (that is, literature) can convincingly be looked upon as having a close, organic link with 'sacred' scripture (that is, biblical).

Chaplaincy sermons I usually worked through out-of-doors. I often ventured forth, weather permitting, to settle a schema by the seashore, and seek inspiration amid the joggers, dogs and dog-owners, and the discordant seagulls. Another homiletic route lay around Seaton Park, in the hope that the atmospherics of chattering brook, youngsters at play and St Machar's Cathedral's grandeur would stir my soul. Alas, in my next charge, St Mary's Cathedral, Aberdeen, the walks were to be urban and the pavements crowded, but grey granite and the 'needs must' factor served to focus the mind.

In his discourse *Contra Gentiles* (no. 42), St Athanasius wrote:

> Just as a musician, tuning his lyre and skilfully combining the bass and the sharp notes, the middle and the others, produces a single melody, so the wisdom of God, holding the universe like a lyre, draws together the things in the air with those on earth, and those in heaven with those in the air, and combines the whole with the parts, linking them by his command and will, thus producing in beauty and harmony a single world and a single order within it, while the Word of God remains unmoved with the Father but by his intrinsic being moves everything as seems good to the Father. Everything according to its own nature is given life and subsistence by him, and through him a wonderful and divine harmony is produced.

Occasional thoughts in tune with that lovely passage would enter my mind during rural meanderings connected with the next Sunday's homily.

Thanks to home and other early influences, I have been able to amass, over the years, a private treasure-trove of favourite stanzas, paragraphs, phrases, even half-lines half-remembered, upon which the memory could draw with homiletic discretion. In the Scots College I encouraged the seminarians to be vigilant in their reading and on the watch for material that was arresting, unusual, whimsical or uplifting, since it might one day adorn their homilies with a stimulating thought or fresh insight. The zeal of Sir Arthur Quiller-Couch which he recalls in his Preface to the *Oxford Book of English Verse*, first published in 1900, is relevant: 'To be sure, a man must come to such a task as mine haunted by his youth and the favourites he loved when he had much enthusiasm but little reading.' Enthusiasm: a fitting word, whose root meaning suggests inspiration from a godly source, in our case the Deity himself. Another eminent don, G. M. Trevelyan, in his Clark Lectures at Cambridge in 1953 entitled *A Layman's Love of Letters*, spoke with affection of authors like Robert Browning, Meredith and Houseman, and deplored that academic approach to literature which sees it as a set of intellectual conundrums. Trevelyan describes it rather as 'joy, joy in our inmost hearts'.[2]

The *Oxford Reference Dictionary* defines literature thus: 'written works, especially those valued for their beauty of form and style'. We may compare that with Professor Boyle's dictum: 'Literature is language free from instrumental purpose, and it seeks to tell the truth'. The two definitions are not contradictory. Indeed 'beauty of form and style' is common to 'sacred' and 'secular' scripture alike. The illuminating position held by Boyle is, as we have seen (Chs. 1 and 4), that 'sacred' and 'secular' scriptures are concerned with truth – the expression of it in the Bible, the quest for it going beyond the Bible. Moreover, there is a twofold snare against which we must guard: first, to grant to literature, however fine, 'purposiveness' which Boyle rules out in his insistence that 'the defining feature of secular literature is its non-instrumental use of words in order to give enjoyment'; and second, to let the glories of the biblical 'script' distract us from learning the lessons, appreciating the teaching emerging from that script for our own and others' spiritual good.

As for the contentious question about the merits of English translations of the Bible, here is one Daniel who will shrink from entering that particular leonine den. I once asked a distinguished scholar, Dermot Cox, OFM, of the Gregorian University, what he thought about the accuracy of the Authorized Version. 'Oh, it's excellent,' he replied, 'with no more mistakes than most of the modern versions.' So perhaps our acerbic friar had a more poetic bent than was apparent.

Clearly our use of literature in preaching must be flexible. What excites one priest or minister may leave another unmoved. In garnishing our homiletic fare with literary references that 'seek to tell the truth' there should be sensitivity, restraint, and pastoral awareness. Again and again, Fr Robert Hendrie (a priest of the Archdiocese of St Andrews and Edinburgh), in his recent book *Go, Tell Them*, reminds us homilists of the necessity of being attuned to the nature and needs of a particular parish. The priest has to do the adapting, not the people. Fr Hendrie has no time for the unseasonably learned preacher. He declares:

> That there will always be someone in the congregation who knows more than he does can be his caution. As the bottom line, he should know enough to know the limits of his knowledge and preserve himself and the Church from ridicule. Like Socrates, he should know that he does not know everything and that that is nothing to be ashamed of.[3]

Certainly the finest communicators whom I have encountered – Bishop Richard Holloway, say, or Very Rev. Archie Craig, or Mgr Ronald Knox (whose sermon collections still delight, not least those first given to schoolchildren) – have never been guilty of condescension. Rather touchingly, there was an Aberdeen minister, James Wood, a frequent contributor to Radio

Scotland's *Ere I Sleep*, who would jot down on the corner of his script the names of those he wished to remember in the course of each broadcast.

Mindful always of the sub-title given to this book, 'The use of literature as a practical aid to preaching', I have to be clear about the way in which the two areas, 'use of literature' and 'a practical aid' intertwine. I would opine that the use of literature should, as it were, furnish the condiments of the feast, not the substance. Condiments have their place both literally and metaphorically, but must be admixed with discretion. Over-spiced fare, as described in Sydney Smith's *Winter Salad*, must be avoided:

> Of mordant mustard, add a single spoon,
> Distrust a condiment that bites too soon;
> But deem it not, thou man of herbs, a fault,
> To add a double quantity of salt;
> Three times the spoon with oil of Lucca crown,
> And once with vinegar, produced from town ...[4]

Distrust a condiment which bites too soon. *Meden agan* ('nothing to excess'), as the inscription in the temple of Delphi warned the ancient Greeks!

It should be remembered that while the above references to 'condiments' and 'feast' are justifiable, they must be seen in the context of the liturgy as a whole. The word 'liturgy' (Greek *leitourgia*) implies public worship. A deeper involvement in public worship will come for clergy and congregation the more that not only literature, but the Arts in general, are available to them. Aidan Kavanagh, in his book *On Liturgical Theology*, goes even further:

Liturgy happens only in the rough and tumbled landscape of spaces and times which people discover and quarry for meaning in their lives. This is an artistic enterprise ... A liturgical scholar who is illiterate in the several human arts can never know his or her subject adequately.[5]

And within a remarkable pamphlet called *Preaching Basics*, derived for the most part from the US Bishops' 1982 publication, *Fulfilled in Your Hearing*, a section on the Arts has this to say:

Worship and the Arts are intimately related. *Environment and Art in Catholic Worship* puts it well: 'God does not need liturgy, people do, and people have only their own arts and styles of expression with which to celebrate.' Over the centuries the liturgy has been a fount of artistic inspiration. It has moved builders to construct great cathedrals, composers to write enthralling music and craftspeople to shape beautiful vessels or design delicate glasswork. It has also inspired preachers over the centuries to ply their craft for the glory of God and the sanctification of the faithful.[6]

Quoting *Fulfilled in Your Hearing* again (section 32), our *multum in parvo* booklet continues: 'Regular and sustained contact with the world's greatest literature or with its painting, sculpture and musical achievements can rightly be regarded by preachers not simply as a leisure-time activity but as part of their ongoing professional development.' Homilists hungry for fresh ideas, the pamphleteer goes on, need only immerse themselves in the arts, for 'there they will find an often unexplored and virtually inexhaustible bounty'. And the concise summing-up is given thus:

Preachers are not expected to be connoisseurs or aesthetes. Season tickets to the opera or symphony do not a preacher make (sic!). On the other hand, preachers are required to develop their imaginations, grow in their understanding of culture and tradition, and acquaint themselves with the people to whom they minister.[7]

What is written above is true and reaffirming, but two strict conditions have to be attached to the use of every homiletic quotation: that the preacher himself fully understands the import of what the author has written, and that he (or she) is as certain as can be that the meaning is likely to be grasped by the majority of those who hear it. Hence, for example, foreign expressions would smack of preciosity (outside College or University circles), and recondite allusions to the Church Fathers or quotations from difficult contemporary theologians would be unacceptable. Minds of the calibre of St Athanasius in his day or T. F. Torrance in ours were perhaps more graced with the gifts of insight than of communication! Preaching is concerned with directness and clarity, so the obscurantism or polemics of Academe are inappropriate to a parochial assembly. As one wag put it, the problem about this is not (*pace* Milton) 'the hungry sheep look up and are not fed', but 'the hungry sheep look up, not too well-read'!

Hymn books can be useful reference points. Introducing his *Penguin Book of Hymns*, Dr Ian Bradley wrote: 'Hymns are perhaps the strongest expression of the folk-religion which is still deeply embedded in our so-called secular society ... for many people they provide a more familiar and accessible source of teaching about the Christian faith than the Bible.'[8] Indeed the long success of *Songs of Praise* on BBC television and of *Sunday Half-Hour* on Radio 2 bears out his statement.

The question does arise for us, however: how many hymns can be classed as literature? What of the great Anglican compositions of the nineteenth century, or the glorious Methodist tradition? Hymns' effectiveness rests upon their spiritual force and literary grace; and where fine music accompanies, how lovely the combination. The point is famously affirmed by George Herbert:

> The fineness which a hymn or psalm affords,
> Is when the soul unto the lines accords.[9]

Arguments rage about the worth and standard of much current hymn writing, but this observer will not cavil. Dr Bradley wonders whether some hymns should be explained within services.[10] I would even suggest that, now and again, a retrospective preachment might be made over a hymn just sung, particularly where it is Bible-based and in accord with the readings of the day. For instance, *Come, Holy Ghost, our souls inspire* (*Veni, Creator Spiritus*) would be a good foundation for a Pentecost homily. In Part II of this book I include a similar approach with Newman's *Lead, kindly light*.

Turning to prose passages, the scale is huge and the variety all but infinite. A personal litany of favourite passages would not advance this book's purposes, but I will briefly dare to mention three superb anthologies that have appealed over the years to my Autolycus-like investigations.[11]

The first, *A Little Book of Life and Death*,[12] has been reprinted times without number. Among its contributors many are now forgotten or disregarded – William Penn, say, or Dora Greenwell, but they form part of my private 'treasure-trove', and have proved useful. The little book's range is wide, encompassing the needs of humankind from the cradle to the grave. It would repay the diligence of a determined mole in 'remainder' religious bookstalls.

The second anthology is more recent, published in 1995 by SPCK as *The Book of Christian Prayer*. It moves freely from approaches to prayer on the one hand to meditations on the Christian Year on the other. This extract ('In times of temptation', of unknown Celtic origin), cries out for homiletic inclusion:

> My thoughts can cross an ocean with a single leap; they can fly from earth to heaven, and back again, in a single second ... No chain, no locks can hold them back; no threats of punishment can restrain them, no hiss of a lash can frighten them. They slip from my grasp like tails of eels; they swoop hither and thither like swallows in flight.

The novelist Elizabeth Goudge's anthology of prose and poetry, first published by Collins in 1964, has consoled many.[13] Among its more sombre surprises is a poignant prayer by Dietrich Bonhoeffer for his fellow-prisoners in a concentration camp, and Humbert Wolfe's lines from his *Uncelestial City* about a charwoman going about her work, aware that the hour has come for her son to be hanged for murder. Compassionate preachers could profitably absorb passages of this kind.

By way of a brief addendum to my three preferred anthologies I would mention the work of Caryll Houselander, especially her meditations on the Way of the Cross,[14] as inspired as they are inspiring. The prayers she adds after each 'station' are perfect. Here is part of the one following 'Jesus is laid in the sepulchre': 'Grant to us all, Lord Jesus, that in the soul's long winters, we may wait patiently, grow imperceptibly in the rhythms and seasons of your love, and so enter into your peace.' That has indeed style and beauty but, more significantly, it seeks to tell the truth.

In any longer exposition of my choices few contemporary pieces would occur. With certain exceptions (the books of Henri Nouwen in particular) my literary and musical periods would coincide, the latter's *terminus ad quem* coming with Elgar and Stravinsky. Ears and eyes must be alert to fresh delights, of course, but there are no friends like the old friends.

With regard to drama, its homiletic uses are constricted, often because plucking out lines from the context of a play could be misleading (Shakespeare generally excepted); also, where the dialogue is in 'ordinary' speech, it is hard to isolate lines without destroying their relevance to a given scene or action. Verse-drama is rather a different case. The plays of Christopher Fry and T. S. Eliot are rich resources (for example, the former's *A Sleep of Prisoners* and the latter's *Murder in the Cathedral*). Dylan Thomas's *Under Milk Wood* is another brilliant exemplar.

One of the lectures given in Aberdeen University (January 2008) within a series called *The Career and Prospects of Providence in Modern Theology* brought me as a homilist much joy. In it, Dr Francesca Murphy compared and contrasted the role of Providence in the life of King David in 1 Samuel and in the personality of Hamlet. Here was 'sacred' and 'secular' scripture connected in a practical union of which even Nicholas Boyle might approve! We shall see in the next chapter how he deals with *The Tempest* with yet more insights.

The poetic canvas is vast also. Yet from the homilist's point of view it is easier to pick out an individual plum there than it is in a prose-garden. Within a fine poem, long or short, it is the single line or couplet that will elicit from the preacher and the people stimulus and appreciation.

It should be stressed again that flexibility is of the essence; in the words of the Latin tag, *De gustibus non est disputandum* ('there is no room for argument where tastes are concerned'). The preacher's personality, the nature of the parish, the tradition (pastoral and historical) of the church, the level of education among the folk – these are but a few of the variables. On the educational side especial sensitivity is required.

I will permit myself a little more space for poetry than I did in referring to prose selections. I think I am of the same mind as Matthew Arnold who, in his *Essays in Criticism* (Thomas Gray): wrote 'The difference between genuine poetry and the poetry of Dryden, Pope, and all their school, is briefly this: their poetry is conceived and composed in their wits, genuine poetry is conceived and composed in the soul.' A matter of *gravitas*, evidently. Chief among my private 'greats' are Gray's *Elegy written in a Country Churchyard*, Tennyson's *In Memoriam*, Wordsworth's *Ode on the Intimations of Immortality*, Arnold's *Sohrab and Rustum* and (if the latter will allow!) Dryden's *Ode for St Cecilia's Day*, clearly 'conceived and composed in the soul'.

On my solitary meanderings, I have had to be careful lest douce Aberdonian passers-by, observing me 'muttering my wayward fancies' might think I was 'nae wise'! One day, puffing my way on a hot day up Seaton Park's ascent to St Machar's Cathedral, an astonished student, on his way back to Hall, overheard my breathless rendering of Christina Rossetti's *Does the road wind uphill all the way?* and wondered.

Twentieth-century poets whose work has found its way into my preaching include John Betjeman, Ralph Hodgson, A. E. Housman, Ted Hughes and John Masefield. Some of the First World War poets have helped too – notably Edward Thomas, Isaac Rosenberg and, above all, Wilfred Owen. Two widely differing clergymen have moved me greatly – Gerard Manley Hopkins (see also Ch. 3), and R. S. Thomas from Wales. Each seems to vacillate between doubt and certainty of faith and between anger and contentment, though their religious traditions and backgrounds were totally different. That both suffered from some form of clinical depression is hardly in doubt, though some would argue that some of their finest verses arose out of the darker experiences of their lives. The so-called 'terrible sonnets' of Hopkins, written probably in 1885, are referred to in a letter of September 1st of that year to Robert Bridges:

> I shall shortly have some sonnets to send you, five or more ... And in the life I lead now, which is one of a continually jaded and harassed mind, if in any leisure I try to do anything I make no way – nor with my work, alas! but so it must be.[15]

Mercifully both poets have brighter episodes, and one of Thomas's where the verse is rich and the theme biblical, *The Bright Field*, demands a full quotation: I have used its brief entirety as the basis of an evening sermon preached to Catholic students in King's College chapel:

I have seen the sun break through
To illuminate a small field
For a while, and gone my way
And forgotten it. But that was the pearl
of great price, the one field that had
the treasure in it. I realize now
that I must give all that I have
to possess it. Life is not hurrying
on to a receding future, nor hankering after
an imagined past. It is the turning
aside like Moses to the miracle
of the lit bush, to a brightness
that seemed as transitory as your youth
once, but is the eternity that awaits you.[16]

It may be asked how the melancholic moods of those
two poets, and of the war-poets, for example, accord with
Professor Boyle's contention that secular literature
exploits writing in order to give pleasure, to entertain.
The response has itself to be Boylian. The point is made,
that when we find 'pleasure' in the sadder experiences of
humanity, it derives from the consolation that is the
sharing of grief. 'We share the pain,' says Boyle, 'of
knowing a truth about our shared condition.' That seems
to me to be a key consideration. Some might feel easier
in describing as 'emotional identity' what Boyle calls
'pleasure'.[17]

On the Scottish front, Burns has his place, subject to
sound, not prudish selection; so do some of the old
ballads. Homiletically apt are some of R. L. Stevenson's
verses – childlike, never childish. Edwin Muir, Norman
McCaig and George Mackay Brown are among more
modern Scots brimful of homiletic possibilities.

A personal trawl through the American poets would

reveal for my preaching purposes three in particular: Emily Dickinson, Robert Frost and E. E. Cummings. Take the latter's quasi-Franciscan salute to a lovely morning:

> I thank you God for this most amazing
> Day: for the leaping greenly spirits of trees
> and a blue true dream of sky; and for everything
> which is natural which is infinite which is yes.[18]

'. . . the leaping greenly spirits of trees' – oh, it cries out for inclusion in an Easter homily!

Emily Dickinson's aquatic glimpse of the after-life is a special gem among many:

> We thirst at first – 'tis Nature's Act –
> And later – when we die –
> A little water supplicate –
> Of fingers going by –
> It intimates the finer want –
> Whose adequate supply
> Is that Great Water in the West –
> Termed immortality.[19]

Imagine the impact those lines could have at the conclusion of a funeral homily.

Is it, on the other hand, ever safe to use humour in preaching, when commonsense and appropriateness would seem to suggest it? My reply would be negative, except in the case of a proven practitioner, and even then only rarely. Many a young preacher has been shipwrecked upon the treacherous shoals of comedy. Rarely, I think, have I been guilty myself, though I do recall reading Belloc's *Matilda* to a pupils' Assembly at

Aberdeen Grammar School in an effort to buttress their truthfulness, and they evidently liked it!

In summation, I offer three slants on preaching. The first is from the *Introduction to Fellowship* papers of the College of Preachers, where the editor states:

> It is said that preaching generally is diving towards delta. The aim of the College of Preachers is to put it upwards towards alpha. This means rekindling the flames. It means convincing clergy and readers that preaching is still significant and powerful. It matters ... Preaching, I believe, is an art form.[20]

The second slant derives from Yves Congar, in his implied thoughts about 'reception' on the part of preacher and listener. Rolando V. De La Rosa, OP, opines that 'Congar's description of tradition as "not merely a transmission followed by a passive, mechanical reception but entails the making present in a human consciousness of a saving truth" aptly describes (*mutatis mutandis*) the preaching event as well.' That 'consciousness of a saving truth' chimes well with Nicholas Boyle's much-quoted contention about literature's seeking, as secular scripture, to tell the truth.[21]

The third slant comes from *Colloquia Peripatetica* – notes of conversations with John Duncan, Professor of Hebrew in New College, Edinburgh, fully a century ago, when pulpit-preaching was at its peak:

> I like direct, practical preaching, which helps me to live as a pilgrim on a journey. Now some preach as if they were telling how to make shoes, instead of making them, as if they were describing the process of shoemaking to those who want to be shod. They would have their hearers all taught to be capital shoemakers, while you want to be a

shoe-wearer. They tell you all about the leather, and the resin, and the awl; while it's a rough road for bare feet and cold that you must travel constantly.[22]

In this chapter I have tried not to pontificate about shoemaking, about foot-comfort or fashion. I have merely sought to promote one optional factor in preaching – the literary one – without favouring brogued footwear over plain or vice versa. The shoe is really the same shoe, and the task facing us the same, however we preach. And the One we wish to serve, whose word we would proclaim, is the same One the latchet of whose shoe we are not worthy to unloose.

A far lesser foot and shoe is Shakespeare's, but he is literature's nonpareil and will dominate my final chapter. Aided by Professor Boyle, who looks at the 'revelatory' force of literature in a scene from *The Tempest,* other Shakespearian productions at Stratford-on-Avon are examined in the same light. Attention will be given to that 'extinction of personality', that 'pure writtenness' evident in the finest authors, a vital element in their enabling the 'revelatory' nature of literature to shine through unimpeded. The chapter will conclude with thoughts on style and on the need for personal holiness in the homilist.

Notes

1. Horace, *Epistles* II, 2, 45.
2. Trevelyan, G. M., *A Layman's Love of Letters* (Longmans, Green & Co., London, 1954).
3. Hendrie, *Go, Tell Them*, p. 196.
4. Quoted in *The Smith of Smiths*, ed. Hesketh Pearson (The Folio Society, London, 1977), p. 229.

5. Kavanagh, A., *On Liturgical Theory* (The Liturgical Press, Collegeville, Minnesota, 1984), p. 139.
6. Foley, E., *Preaching Basics: A Model and a Method* (Archdiocese of Chicago, Liturgy Training Publications, Chicago, 1998), pp. 16–17.
7. Ibid.
8. *The Penguin Book of Hymns*, ed. I. Bradley (Penguin Books Ltd., 1990), p. 2.
9. Herbert, 'A true hymn'.
10. Bradley, p. 4.
11. 'A snapper-up of unconsidered trifles'; Shakespeare, *The Winter's Tale*, IV, 2, 26.
12. *A Little Book of Life and Death*, ed. E. Waterhouse (Methuen, London, 1902).
13. Goudge, E., *Book of Comfort*.
14. Houselander, C., *The Stations of the Cross* (Hart Books, London, 1955).
15. Hopkins, p. 249.
16. Thomas, R. S., *Collected Poems*, p. 302.
17. Boyle, p. 130.
18. Cummings, E. E., *Complete Poems*, Vol. II (Granada, London, 1962), p. 663.
19. Dickinson, E., *The Complete Poems*, ed. T. H. Johnson (Faber & Faber, London, 1975), p. 726.
20. Publication privately circulated to members.
21. Quoted in *Grace and Task of Preaching*, p. 132.
22. *Colloquia Peripatetica*, 1.

Chapter 6

'O Brave New World'

*Dost thou not know what a passion for sermons has
burst in upon the minds of Christians nowadays? And
that those who practise themselves in preaching are in
especial honour, not only among the heathen, but among
them of the household of the faith?*[1]

Enthused by those words of St John Chrysostom, I begin
my final chapter. Nearer now to four-score years than
three, I shall avoid morose retrospection in favour of
practical rumination. I have divided my final thoughts
into three sections: the first reflects on aspects of
Shakespearean drama in the light of Professor Boyle's
approach to literature (cf. Chapter 1); the second upon
matters of style; and the third on the importance of the
preacher's personal spirituality.

That Boyle should have elected to focus on *The
Tempest* helps us to pin down his theorizing and move
towards a practical understanding of it.[2] Pursuing his
conviction about the 'revelatory' role of literature, he
maintains that 'fiction' in the widest sense 'puts into
words or into mimic show things that, before we heard
and saw them, we did not know we knew'. That statement
is crucial to the development of my own offerings. He
continues:

so for example, there are many fine things said and shown
in *The Tempest* about art and age and resentment and drink

and, possibly, colonialism. We recognize their truth and so recognize in the text the world we all share. But what makes the play almost a revelation is – to borrow a term from painting as much as music – its tonality, the unique harmony of its many voices, audible for a moment perhaps ... in the exchange between Miranda and Prospero, the moment in which the text springs its surprise:

> Miranda: O brave new world
> That has such people in't!
> Prospero: 'Tis new to thee.[3]

'In those few words,' Boyle writes,

> and in the spectacle of the stained and sorry crew that call forth Miranda's exclamation, innocence and appetite and love and generosity and promise are married up with experience and disillusion and comedy and maturity and forgiveness, and the whole 'world' – as the characters call it – is seen in a light at once multiple and strangely clear, like a landscape after the storm that gives the play its title.

One cannot but share the excitement of Boyle's insight here, especially when he adds this, the defining point of his argument:

> The world which is seen in the light of this dialogue is the world of the text – the world of *this* text, the play named after the storm ... We identify it historically and even biographically as his [Shakespeare's] world, or at least as the world of this particular play. But there is another world still that the words of Miranda and Prospero let us glimpse, behind even the world of the text, another world about which the play is telling us – or allowing us to sense – the truth. It is not the world that has such people in it ... it is the world that has such texts in it, that has amongst other things *The Tempest* in it and us, *The Tempest*'s audience.

The world in which the understanding and desire and growth in forgiveness that the world of *The Tempest* contains is a representation or imitation, a miming, of what we all acknowledge to be, not life as seen by Shakespeare, but just life. At such a moment the play is as near as it can be to revelation of a truth, and Shakespeare is simply the instrument who has provided the words without which we could not have uttered or named it. The play has become a secular scripture.[4]

Professor Boyle appends this key affirmation:

The truth the play presents to us is that there is truth, that is to say, that life can reveal itself in words; that there is life, and that there is knowledge, and that the rule of right knowing and right living are the same ... It [*The Tempest*] speaks truly of truth and so is poised on the verge of pure writtenness, pure independence of its author.

The last point is made also by T. S. Eliot: 'What happens is a continual surrender of himself [the poet], as he is at the moment, to something which is more valuable. The progress of an artist is a continual self-sacrifice, a continual extinction of personality.'[5] I am persuaded that the claim that life can reveal itself in words has been sustained by Boyle.

Personal experience of innumerable Shakespearean productions over the years reinforces the case made above. Certain performances are unforgettable – Wolfit's Lear, Falstaff and Touchstone; the Edith Evans/Godfrey Tearle *Antony and Cleopatra*; a quartet of Hamlets – Redgrave, Bannen, Warner and Courtenay; and Derek Jacobi's moving creation of the neurotic and wayward Richard II. I have seen *The Tempest* only once, a rather ordinary production except for Alistair Sim's Prospero, outstanding in presence and diction. The Prospero in Stratford some forty years ago was the late Tom Fleming, a friend for twenty-five years. Too reticent about his achievements, his racy reminiscences were a treat! And now there is Antony Sher's interpretation to look forward to at the Courtyard Theatre (January–March, 2009).

During their extended season of 2006–2007, the Royal Shakespeare Company put on the entire canon of the Bard's plays. My tally was four, but I came away from them more sure than ever of the rightness of Nicholas Boyle's tenets about 'secular scripture'. This will not mean that homiletic quotations from *Romeo and Juliet*, *Julius Caesar*, *Richard III* and *Twelfth Night* will superabound, but it should mean that Shakespeare's 'mirror up to nature' dictum[6] will help me to approach the wholeness of life, and truth, and the consequent 'revelation' in my preaching with confidence and conviction.

Here are illustrations from each of the four plays in turn. A brief scene from *Romeo and Juliet* will do – the opening of Act III, scene 5, the two lovers being 'aloft' with the ladder of cords. That the 'aloft' scenario was dependent upon some highly contemporary metal scaffolding, rather than the balcony of a villa, had to be ignored. It is near daybreak, and Romeo must flee, but the dialogue as to whether it really is dawn yet is a masterly depiction not only of the heady unreasonableness of a couple deeply in love, or of the humour the audience may derive from it, but also of the hopelessness and potential tragedy looming for the two young people caught up in a mesh of family feuds and intrigue. Moreover, typically in such circumstances, the playwright invests his lines with the loveliest blank verse, for example, Juliet's 'It is the lark that sings so out of

tune, Straining harsh discords and unpleasing sharps.'
Small wonder that musicians of the calibre of
Tchaikovsky and Prokofiev were drawn into their own
harmonies around the theme.

Julius Caesar was played in such a way as to engage
the audience in contemporary reflections about tyranny
and political manipulation. One's sympathies were
enlisted now with Caesar himself, now with Brutus, now
even with Cassius at the close of the famous 'quarrel
scene' with his friend. Mark Antony, played by an
African actor, succeeded in coupling the 'ideal' character,
as popularly perceived, with the ruthless, traitorous
opportunist. There is so much reflected from the 'mirror'
of that play to make us all feel nervy and guilty. Life's
seamier side must be acknowledged, and we are sadly
contributors to it. Homilists need not dig deep to uncover
it. Cassius's enticement of Brutus into the ranks of the
conspirators illustrates a political chicanery evident in
seventeenth-century England and apparent in our time
too, not only in the developing world but in Western
democracies as well. This smear upon Caesar by Cassius
has its parallels in current political experience:

> He had a fever when he was in Spain,
> And when the fit was on him, I did mark
> How he did shake. 'Tis true, this god did shake.
> His coward lips did from their colour fly...[7]

Performances of *Richard III* are not for the
fainthearted, and last year's Stratford production in the
Courtyard Theatre was predictably gory and gruesome.
Of the three Richards I have seen (Donald Wolfit and
Christopher Plummer being the earlier), this one –

Jonathan Slinger – was the most subtle. With reference to this study and to its concern with the scripture-literature syndrome, the baseness to which humanity can sink was unsparingly portrayed and my mind occasionally wandered to incidents in the Old Testament, where even the Lord's anointed could be cruel and crafty.

The admixture of good and evil conduct in humanity presents many challenges to Shakespeare's creativity, and is also, alas, only too readily detectable within ourselves. Take *Richard III*: The Duke of Clarence's career was far from spotless, but his end – to be drowned in a butt of malmsey – is unspeakably appalling. His account of the previous night's awful dream attains to glorious lyrical heights – often Shakespeare's way when doom is imminent. Here is an excerpt:

> O Lord! Methought what pain it was to drown,
> What dreadful noise of waters in my ears,
> What sights of ugly death within my eyes.
> Methought I saw a thousand fearful wrecks,
> Ten thousand men that fishes gnawed upon,
> Wedges of gold, great ouches, heaps of pearl,
> Inestimable stones, unvalued jewels,
> All scattered in the bottom of the sea.[8]

Considered more as tragedy than history, there is evidence of that catharsis (purification) of which Aristotle speaks in this genre, and of the 'pity and terror' he regards as central. It is conspicuous in the episode above.

The fourth production to be seen was *Twelfth Night*, a play I first encountered and enjoyed at school. The troubles with the Stratford performance arose mainly from the self-indulgence of the producer (Neil Bartlett).

He had the principal comic characters (Sir Toby Belch and Sir Andrew Aguecheek) and their assistant, Fabian, played by women, and the heroine, Viola, by a man!

My reaction to this was unease, an unease shared by a few of the professional critics. The *Daily Telegraph*[9] scathingly reproached Mr Bartlett for the liberties taken, while in *The Guardian*[10] Michael Billington wrote: 'A programme note by Alan Sinfield implies the intention is to heighten awareness of "the general instability of gender roles in our time". If that is the real aim, I would suggest that Joe Orton does it better.'

The brilliant cast nevertheless produced a tour-de-force by dint of accomplished professionalism, clear diction, and, despite the eccentricities, an effective demonstration of teamwork. The Malvolio was superb, one reviewer remarking, 'even his walk implies he disdains the ground he treads on'! He led the ensemble in a way that revealed the play's darker moments and incidents without detracting from either its romantic or comic scenes. My discourse is indebted to Shakespeare for the light this play shines upon human nature – its absurdities, its tenderness, its spirit of final reconciliation – in a word, its 'revelatory' role in showing up truths about the human condition. Perhaps above all, the text's three songs, sung by Feste, indicated with charming profundity areas of experience that punctuated the action: 'O mistress mine' (young love and longing); 'Come away, come away, death' (mortality and despair): and 'When that I was and a tiny little boy' (the ages of man and the fleetingness of time). I would argue that from those songs alone a homilist could develop useful pastoral material.

There was a fifth performance at Stratford that came my way, though I venture to assess its worth and content

with some caution. It was *Merry Wives The Musical*
(sic!). It seemed rather long-drawn-out, a curate's egg of
an affair. Much of the text was retained, frequently
disrupted by unremarkable songs. Still, nothing could
obliterate the play's delights, and the acting was of high
merit. The pure 'writtenness' still shone through, and it
was perfectly possible to enter the 'world' of the action,
and to identify with aspects of human quirkiness that are
timeless and ring true. The words were best pointed by
Dame Judi Dench (wobbly, however, in her singing's
upper register!), and by Simon Callow, whose quip about
Falstaff's submersion in the Thames, 'I have a kind of
alacrity in sinking', brought the house down and of itself
justified the astronomical ticket price.

Whether the enterprise was justified in this form is
debatable. At any rate, Matthew Arnold's famous sonnet,
Shakespeare, which includes a reference to the great
man's smiling, suggests that the playwright would readily
pardon the Stratfordian revels in question. The sonnet's
quatrain beginning 'Planting his steadfast footsteps in the
sea' leads one commentator[11] to find in it a reminiscence
of Cowper's hymn, *God moves in a mysterious way*, the
third line of which runs, 'He plants his footsteps in the
sea', and an implied parallel in Schiller:[12] 'Like Deity
behind the universe, he [that is, the 'objective' poet of
Shakespeare's kind] hides himself behind his work.' That
sentence accords with T. S. Eliot's and Nicholas Boyle's
views about the 'extinction of personality' achievable by
the finest authors.

Shakespeare at the summit, undoubtedly – 'Thou
smilest and art still,' says Arnold, 'out-topping
knowledge.' Dickens is at or near the summit when it
comes to the novel, and Boyle's remarks about him

accord with his over-all proposition: 'literature is language free of instrumental purpose, and it seeks to tell the truth'.[13] Such, he maintains, are the twin premises of a Catholic approach to literature, whether sacred or secular. His contention is more than persuasive to me; it is compelling.

Between the above remarks about literature and subsequent comments about a preacher's personal holiness, there follow some brief thoughts about style. Robert McCracken, writing fifty years ago, said:

> It is a misfortune when a preacher has no feeling for the magic of words and no flair for word-weaving. We should care for words, select them judiciously and lovingly ... The fact of the matter is that most of us do our writing and speaking in clichés, in trite hackneyed and stereotyped phrases. We should cultivate the sense of the sound, value and association of words, of individual words. The truth merits the noblest expression we can give it.[14]

Those words echo Petronius Arbiter's compliment to Horace on his *curiosa felicitas dictionis* ('judicious felicity of expression').[15]

Not that homilists are required to be grammarians, but they must master, or have mastered, the basic principles of good communication – clarity, cogency, conviction and audibility. A fine exemplar at present is Barak Obama, whose speeches have been linked even in the media to 'poetry' or 'like those of a preacher'. The sorry fact is that far too few of our homilists (at least in my Church) are adequately equipped for their task.

This is not the place to give guidelines, but I will offer a few reflections of others with greater expertise. First is a formidable American divine, Grenville Kleiser, who

long ago averred: 'It would startle one into serious
thinking to hear a leading New York clergyman assert, as
one did recently, that there are too many messageless
sermons, and that the preachers fail to teach truths of
which people stand in greatest need.'[16] He adds,
however: 'perfection of English style, rhetorical
floridness, and profundity of thought will never wholly
make up for lack of appropriate action in the work of
persuading men.' No; but perfection of English style (or
the desire to strive for it, at any rate) need not be
divorced from the 'appropriate' action either. And our
author has this curious advice, not contained in any other
manual I can find:

> The effectiveness of the whisper in preaching should not be
> overlooked. If discreetly used it may serve to impress the
> hearer with the profundity and seriousness of the preacher's
> message, or to arrest and bring back to the point of contact
> the wandering minds of a congregation.

A by-product of style worth pondering by any man
questing for 'a practical aid to preaching'! Quite how our
author's essay on sermonizing fits in with the book's title,
How to Argue and Win is hard to see. A homily can never
be an argument, and woe betide the homilist who even
appears to flirt with triumphalism!

Hilaire Belloc's claim that 'no man of letters dares to
whisper that letters themselves are not often much more
than a pastime to the reader, and are only very rarely
upon a level with good and serious speculation'[17] is not a
contradiction of what we have found in the weighty words
of Boyle: 'a book becomes literature by using language
for the purposeless purpose of enjoyment.'

That discerning literary critic, Robert Lynd, writing

some seventy years ago, recalled his readers to due
reverence for well-written work, and we preachers ignore
such counsel at our peril. Here are his words:

> Literature maintains an endless quarrel with idle sentences
> ... It would not matter if it were only the paunched and flat-
> footed authors who were proclaiming the importance of
> writing without style. Unhappily, many excellent writers as
> well have used their gift of style to publish the praise of
> stylelessness ... Perhaps it is not quite fair to call it the
> heresy of stylelessness; it would be more accurate to
> describe it as the heresy of style without pains.[18]

Lynd continues with a reflection which could be a
salutary reminder to the preaching fraternity: 'Style is a
method, not of decoration, but of expression. It is an
attempt to make the beauty and energy of the imagination
articulate.'[19] There is no question of recommending
pompous or high-sounding effusion for its own sake, but
there can be a rightful place for Horace's dictum:

> *inceptas gravibus plerumque et magna professis*
> *Purpureus, late quae splendeat, unus et alter*
> *Adsuitur pannus.*[20]
> ('Often on a work of grave purpose and high promise
> is tacked a purple patch or two to give an effect
> of colour.')

Not for all homilists, this guidance, but where would
we be without the colour *and* rhetorical talents of many
who have gone before us, and for a few, in our own
time, capable of empurpling their preaching likewise?
Aeschylus's line occurs in this connection:[21] 'Words are
physic to the distempered mind.'

Even the most gifted orators must, all the same, be

humble, bearing in mind the sage advice of St John Chrysostom: 'Preaching is not a natural but acquired power; though a man may reach a high standard, even then his power may forsake him unless he cultivate it by constant application and exercise.'[22]

Wide reading and a love of letters constitute a *sine qua non*. The tiro and the expert alike should hearken to Jonathan Swift:[23] 'Proper words in proper places make the true definition of style.' Or can we infer yet more from the French aphorism of Georges-Louis Leclerc de Buffon, *Le style est l'homme même*? ('Style is the man himself').[24]

Approaching now the latter stages of my argument, we shall examine some aspects of the ordained homilist's spirituality. St Augustine succinctly declares: 'he is a vain preacher of the word of God without, who is not a hearer within.'[25] Even more terse is Chaucer's question within the portrait of the poor Parson: 'If gold rust, what shall iron do?' And still in literary vein, we may apply to our topic Shakespeare's unnerving line: 'Lilies that fester smell far worse than weeds.'[26] As for the liturgy and its Rite of Ordination, the words of the bishop to the prospective priest, whilst the Book of the Gospels is being handed over, could not be clearer: 'Believe what you read, teach what you believe, and practise what you teach.'

Moreover the Church would have us cherish the communication skills we may happen to have, with a view to increasing our confidence as speakers. Timothy Radcliffe, OP, notes of Lacordaire, who refounded the Dominican Order in France after the suppression of religious life in the nineteenth century, how he delighted in his freedom of speech as a preacher:

I have never had a better grasp of freedom than on the day when, together with the blessing of the sacred oils, I received the right to speak of God. The universe then opened up before me, and I realized that in the human being there is something inalienable, divine, and eternally free – the Word.[27]

Holiness, a term suggesting, among other things, set-apartness and dedication to God's service, is the necessary foundation for effective pastoral preaching. Learning, oratory, presentation and all displays of technical excellence are worthless if holiness is absent. The Second Vatican Council's document on the Church, *Lumen Gentium*, states:

> Therefore all in the Church are called to holiness, according to the apostle's saying 'for this is the will of God, your sanctification' (1 Thessalonians IV, 3). This holiness of the Church is expressed in many ways by the individuals who, each in their own state of life, tend to the perfection of charity, and are thus a source of edification for others (V, 39).

And the section concludes: 'Let those who use this world not fix their abode in it, for the form of this world is passing away' (V, 42; cf. 1 Cor. 7:31, Greek text).

Towards achieving this holiness, the Council exhorts us to apply ourselves constantly to prayer, self-denial and active service. The conclusion of Stephen Langton's inaugural lecture in Paris in 1180 bears earlier testimony to that theme:

> What am I going to say, then, seeing as I possess neither an excellent life, nor outstanding knowledge, even as I ascend to the teaching chair? Yet setting my sights upon the

inexhaustible mercy of divine goodness, rather than mere presumption, I now turn my heart and tongue to the service of my Redeemer and commit my purpose and myself to his grace. Amen.[28]

St Francis de Sales suggests, with characteristic gentleness, that, in speaking about God, we should

> let fall the delicious honey of devotion, drop by drop, now in the ear of one, now in the ear of another, praying secretly in your soul that God may let it sink into their hearts ... for it is wonderful how powerfully hearts are moved when goodness is set before them in a fair and lovely guise.[29]

Pace Nicholas Boyle, I am persuaded that one of the uses of literature as a practical aid to preaching lies in the possibility that through its honeyed administration hearts may be moved, when goodness, as our saint suggests, 'is set before them in a fair and lovely guise'. Granted that the scholastic thinkers held that God is 'one, good, true and beautiful' we may leave the first two of those attributes to be dealt with by theologians, but, armed with the philosophical approach of Boyle and the poetic insight of Keats ('Beauty is truth, truth beauty'),[30] we may claim some affinity, through literature, with the third and fourth.

A vivid metaphor is introduced by Daniel Francis, CSsR, thus: 'The pulpit is a mountain. The preaching moment supplies the necessary experience of liminality, the "between-space" or threshold for the encounter with God.' He then quotes the passage in Isaiah 25 beginning, 'On this mountain the Lord of hosts will make for all peoples a feast of fat things ... And he will destroy on this mountain the covering that is cast over all peoples, the veil that is spread over all nations.'[31] The terms 'liminality' and 'between-space' seem appropriate to the preaching ministry whether its source springs from 'sacred' *or* 'secular' scripture. Boyle does appear to be close to such a view when he writes: 'the greatest literature can bring us to the point where we can understand the possibility that the lost Atlantis of Being may reveal itself in words.'[32]

This book's debt to Boyle, and in particular to his clarifying the revelatory relationship of sacred and secular literature, has been immense. The use of literature in preaching can now be regarded not merely as desirable, but as entirely justified. Preaching nonetheless remains at once rewarding and difficult, challenging and wearying, uplifting and frightening. We are vessels of clay, and must needs be humble as we address our task, but God will give the increase.

I hope I may escape the terrible description, 'a louse in the lock of literature',[33] and rejoice rather in these words from Tennyson:

> Our dusted velvets have much need of thee;
> Thou art no sabbath-drawler of old saws,
> Distill'd from some worm-canker'd homily . . .[34]

The homilist's ministry to the person in the pew is one of giving. Fr Robert Hendrie[35] wisely reminds us, however, that 'each hearer adapts the ideas to his or her own use', in accordance with the scholastic saw, *quidquid recipitur ad modum recipientis recipitur* ('whatever is received is received after the manner of the receiver'). He then regales us with this tale and its moral – deserving quotation in full:

Von Hugel once began a lecture to a group of students by asking them to consider tree-frogs. He then told them of one type which swallowed its insect prey lengthwise, but finding this uncomfortable and indigestible, patted its stomach until the unfortunate prey lay crosswise, comfortable – for the frog – and comfortably digested at its own convenience.[36]

Fr Hendrie goes on:

Anyone sharing received meaning with a speaker goes through a similar process of reception, adjustment and absorption – the meaning is now theirs and they can do what they wish with it. Anyone who has been preaching over years can testify to the odd and often uncomfortable ways in which their words sometimes return. [Peter] Drilling appositely quotes Emily Dickinson:[37]

> A Word is dead
> When it is said,
> Some say.
> I say it just
> Begins to live
> That day.[38]

There is ultimate consolation to be found in the final lines of Siegfried Sassoon's poem, *Redemption*:

> I think; if through some chink in me could shine
> But once – but one ray
> From that all-hallowing and eternal day,
> Asking no more of Heaven I would go hence.[39]

Afterword

Mgr Ronald Knox[40] ends one of his spiritual books with words part personal, part Pauline. I choose to borrow them.

> I will not ask pardon for what I have said or what I have left unsaid; God uses our words as he will. I will only ask for your prayers, your charitable prayers, lest perhaps when I have preached to others, I myself should become a castaway.

Notes

1. St John Chrysostom, *On the Priesthood*, V, 8.
2. Boyle, p. 135ff.
3. Act V, 1, 183–4.
4. Boyle, p. 136.
5. From *Tradition and Individual Talent* (1919), quoted in *The MacMillan Anthology of English Prose*, ed. E. Leeson (Papermac, London, 1994), 545.
6. *Hamlet* III, 2, 24.
7. *Julius Caesar* Act II, 2, ll. 124ff.
8. *Richard III*, Act I, 4, ll. 21–8.
9. *The Daily Telegraph*, September 6, 2007.
10. *The Guardian*, September 6, 2007.
11. Allot, K., *The Complete Poems of M. Arnold* (Longman, London, 1965), p. 40.
12. Schiller, F., *Naïve and Sentimental Poetry*, tr. W. F. Maitland (Blackwell, 1951), p. 19.
13. Boyle, pp. 131–3.
14. McCracken, R., *The Making of the Sermon* (S.C.M. Press Ltd., London, 1956), pp. 72–3.
15. Petronius, *Satyricon*, 118, 5.
16. Kleiser, G., *How to Argue and Win* (Funk and Wagnalls, New York 1912), pp. 123, 126, 130.
17. Belloc, H., *On Everything* (Methuen, London, 1910), p. 238.
18. Lynd, R., *The Art of Letters* (Duckworth, London, 1928), pp. 249, 250.

19. Ibid., p. 256.
20. Horace, *Ars Poetica*, 14.
21. Aeschylus, *Prometheus Vinctus*, 380.
22. St John Chrysostom, *On the Priesthood*, V, 5.
23. Swift, J., *Letter to a Young Clergyman*, 9 January 1720.
24. In the essay *Discours sur le Style*.
25. St Augustine, *Sermons*, 129.
26. Shakespeare, Sonnet, no. 94.
27. *Le Père Lacordaire*, by C. de Montalembert (Paris, 1862), quoted by Yves Congar in *La Liberté dans la vie de Lacordaire*.
28. Quoted in C. C. Anderson, *Christian Eloquence: Contemporary Doctrinal Preaching* (Hillenbrand Books, Chicago, 2005), p.173.
29. Francis de Sales, *Introduction to the Devout Life*, III, 26.
30. Keats, J., *Ode on a Grecian Urn*, conclusion.
31. *Theology of Preaching*, p. 89.
32. Boyle, p. 137.
33. Said of J. C. Collins to Edmund Gosse, quoted in E. Charteris, *The Life and Letters of Edmund Gosse* (Heinemenn, 1931), ch. 14.
34. Tennyson, *Sonnet to J.M.K.*
35. Hendrie, *Go, Tell Them*, p. 240.
36. Von Hugel, F., *Essays and Addresses on the Philosophy of Religion*, 1st series (J.M. Dent & Sons, London, 1921), p. 278.
37. *Lonergan Workshop*, Vol. 7 (Scholars Press, Atlanta, Georgia, 1988), p. 99f.
38. Dickinson, E., p. 1212.
39. Sassoon, S., *Sequences* (Faber and Faber, London, 1956), p. 20.
40. Knox, R., *A Retreat for Priests* (Sheed and Ward, London, 1946), p. 185.

Conclusion

Come, sermon me no further (*Timon of Athens* II, 2, 169)

It may be fitting to retrace our steps now in the interests of clarity. It matters that the progression of my thoughts be clear to all.

I started with Timothy Radcliffe's insight into the correlation of the development of words and their preparatory place in awaiting the advent of God's Word. The Bible, he held, does not offer a religious language for speaking to God. It invites us to *converse* with God, to enter into a conversation which stretches open our ways of talking.

Other Dominican thinkers (including Aquinas) see theology, preaching and prayer as 'a response to an earlier expression', and that preaching in particular 'is within the conversation that Father and Son carry on in the Spirit'. Radcliffe brilliantly concludes: 'The Word of God wells up from within human language. The birthpangs of the Word started when the first human beings began to speak.' Then, anticipating what my own reflection would later consider, he opines that 'literature opens our eyes to God's pleasure in his creatures'.

The notion that a preacher may become 'inebriated'

through his encounter with the words of God is developed by Paul Murray, OP, first from the Medieval Hubert of Romans and subsequently from a series of homilists of the Dominican Order.

I have offered Professor Boyle's definition, 'Literature is language free from instrumental purpose, and it seeks to tell the truth', a definition integral to the thrust of my argument. Secular literature, he claims, exploits writing in order to give pleasure, to entertain. Boyle concentrates particularly on poetry (in the broad, Aristotelian sense). Importantly, he states that the pleasure to be had from 'the weaving together of words' can make 'analogues of revelation' capable of illuminating the whole of our life. His insistence that literature is able to tell us the truth about things leads (he argues) to its ability to tell us the truth about Being in general – in other words, how it is capable of amounting to a Revelation. He holds this view in respect of both tragedy and comedy, and concludes that 'representation' (*mimesis* in Aristotle) 'enacts the worth to God of what is represented'. The fact that secular literature is true to life is 'the guarantee that the world of this text is a part of the world we know and inhabit'. In pursuit of this idea, he argues that if we believe the teachings of the Catholic Church to be true statements about human life, then literature that is true to life will corroborate them, be the author Catholic or not. Secular scriptures will be what he calls the prolegomena to the sacred scriptures.

I ended that first chapter with Timothy Radcliffe's homologating Seamus Heaney's view that literature can give us an experience akin to a foreknowledge of certain things which we already seem to be remembering, a view already expressed by Keats:[1] 'Poetry should strike the reader as a wording of his own highest thoughts, and appear almost a remembrance.' Brief quotations from two of R. S. Thomas's poems (*The Answer* and *Where*), concerned with Otherness, had the last word there.

In my second chapter I considered words and the use of words in the light of my personal experiences as a producer of religious programmes on radio and television with BBC Scotland (1969–77), and as Spiritual Director at the Pontifical Scots College in Rome (1977–85). On the broadcasting side, the nature of the work was ecumenical, ranging from simple radio talks to major acts of worship and praise on television. My duties in Rome, essentially on a confidential basis as 'soul-friend' to some fifty ecclesiastical students, involved giving each year-group a spiritual talk every week, into which literary quotations and allusions were regularly introduced, in an attempt to provide the soil, as it were, in which the young men could, if they wished, nurture their own literary flora. Gerard Manley Hopkins' work was a recurring feature.

It fell to the Spiritual Director to supervise the senior students' 'sermon classes' (a term at least better than the 'sacred eloquence' of my own College days!). I encouraged those who wished to add 'secular' to 'sacred' scripture in their homilies (though I did not use that terminology then) to do so by trial and error. At the same time, any student disinclined to veer towards literature was entirely at liberty to choose his own directions. The friendship between mentor and student was greatly helpful in those private pre-preachment sessions where one could work through the student's script or notes constructively and calmly. Every effort was made to avoid 'leaning' on the preacher, and in turn to advise him not to be leant upon by the writers of 'sermon-notes' either in periodicals or on the Internet. I chose to end that chapter with a telling quotation from the Vatican's *Pastoral Instruction on Social Communication*, with whose words my discourse finds itself aligned: 'We are not asking of you that you should play the part of moralists. We are only asking you to have confidence in your mysterious power of opening up the glorious regions of light that lie behind the mystery of man's life.'

Chapter Three, still dependent on Boyle's definition already provided, examined certain passages of prose and poetry that have influenced my own preaching and my approach to it. My choice was intended to suggest how and why some key examples of 'secular' scripture have created one man's awareness of the rich breadth and depth of available material. Boyle maintains that the life that is 'represented' through literature – human life 'warts and all', life indeed as it is watched over by God himself, is affirmed by the act of representation to be worth the labour expended upon it by its author and recognized by the audience of listeners or readers.

My chosen list there reflected different stages of life at which I first encountered them and are, in sequence: Keats, *The Eve of St Agnes*; Bernard Shaw, *St Joan*; Francis Thompson, *The Hound of Heaven*; Charles Dickens, *Martin Chuzzlewit*; Gerard Manley Hopkins, *The Caged Skylark*; Duff Cooper, *Old Men Forget*; and a seventeenth-century anonymous poem about Calvary.

The zealous delight engendered by each extract remains with me still, added to and enriched by innumerable others. The vision, power and truth inherent in them all bears out the force of Boyle's dictum: 'Representation is the moral reality of Redemption projected into the secular realm of pleasure', a dictum as profound as it is succinct.

The previous chapters having concentrated on the literary dimension of my argument, Chapter Four's attention was centred more upon preaching in general. There, I attempted, in other words, to seek out the nature of the soil into which literature is to be homiletically implanted. Using Matthew 28:19-20 as a basis, the command of Jesus to his disciples to 'teach' necessarily seems to incorporate the consequential ministry to 'preach'. The latter is licit under the aegis of the former.

With the support of some estimable authorities, I stressed the need for a good standard of preaching, not least where Catholic homilists are concerned. In the light of the Second Vatican Council's reforms, I examined the homily's role within the structure of the liturgy. Preaching should be part of the priest's or deacon's apostolate as a whole – never a liturgical chore, but rather 'an exciting pastoral opportunity'. I made particular reference to an important sentence from the *Introduction to the Roman Missal* (1974), to the effect that when the Scriptures are read in church God himself speaks to his people and that Christ himself, present in his word, proclaims the gospel. Similar thinking is instanced from the fourth-century *Diatesseron* of Ephraim.

The relationship between 'sacred' and 'secular' scripture came up again. Several literary quotations were given to show how the two strands of scripture may not merely sit comfortably together but also how the 'sacred' may be sharpened and enlivened via the insights of a wide range of authors – poets, playwrights, novelists.

Daniel Francis, CSsR, endorses that view in an essay called *The pulpit is a mountain*. The final sentence from a key passage (quoted in Chapter Four) runs: 'The preaching moment supplies the necessary experience of *liminality* [my italics], the "between-space" or threshold for the encounter with God.' The expression 'liminality' comes as a gift to my reflection, as do its implications. Words from Pope John Paul II's *Pastores Dabo Vobis* are slanted in the same direction. Professor Boyle appears to be of the same mind. After all, if the latter's conviction about literature's function 'to seek to tell the truth' is sound, it cannot but assist in the work of 'drawing back the veil' (Revelation) about the nature of God himself, about enjoying that experience of 'liminality' between earth and heaven.

Chapter Five could not but include some autobiographical material, because an individual's access to both literature and preaching has to depend upon family background, education, experience and taste. I then turned to consider, in the light of the foregoing, some of the 'how' and the 'why' elements in this writer's methodology of preaching, though some words of Athanasius solemnly remind homilists of their total dependence for inspiration upon God, 'while the Word of God remains unmoved with the Father, but by his intrinsic being moves everything as seems good to the Father'.

In trying to express the relationship in a homily between the Bible and literature, the use of literature should, as it were, furnish the condiments of the feast, not the substance. Overspiced fare must be avoided. Some thought is then given to the nature of liturgy (the 'feast') itself, and a historical perspective on the alliance of words, art and even dance in its development. Worship and the Arts have an intimate relationship.

Some space has been given to the importance of hymns within the liturgy, and it seemed fit to suggest that a well-written hymn may be the basis for a homily in itself. To what I referred to as my 'Autolycus-like investigations', there was added a brief survey of three anthologies, mostly of prose, intended to be a guide – no more than that – for anyone aspiring to use literature as a practical aid to preaching. Some 'tasters' in the field of drama are also offered. In the realms of poetry a list that has helped the author is tentatively given, if only to make it clearer upon what literary riches one preacher has unearthed his personal treasury. A quick word is said about the use of humour in preaching, and the chapter ended with three diverse but impressive comments about preaching's part in proclaiming what is true.

The sixth chapter contained at the beginning a penetrating insight by Professor Boyle. What he does is to advance the idea of the 'revelatory' power of literature by examining *The Tempest* by Shakespeare. With special reference to Miranda's famous exclamation: 'O brave new world that has such people in't', Boyle argues that

> the world in which the understanding and desire and growth in forgiveness that the world of *The Tempest* contains is a representation . . . of what we all acknowledge to be, not life as seen by Shakespeare, but just life. At such a moment the play is as near as it can be to revelation of a truth . . . The play has become a secular scripture.

Some points concerning other plays of Shakespeare were made following their production at Stratford-upon-Avon in 2007. Five works were briefly considered, including two 'oddities' – *Twelfth Night*, which the producer cast in a gender-crossed exercise in self-indulgence, and a musical version of *The Merry Wives of Windsor*, scarcely effective despite a star-studded cast including Judi Dench and Alistair McGowan. However, there still came across the happy realization that the text of the plays was 'revelatory' in the Boylian sense, despite the eccentricities of production.

Building on the 'pure writtenness' of Shakespeare, the 'extinction of personality' is achievable by the finest authors. Literature, we have stated again, 'is free of instrumental purpose, and it seeks to tell the truth'.

There followed some remarks about the importance of a sound familiarity with style. This was not by way of offering personal guidelines, but rather to encourage or reaffirm homilists in the light of the wisdom of our predecessors, including Belloc and Robert Lynd, neither of them preachers, yet capable of a shrewd assessment of others' style in any field of writing.

The final consideration examined in this book has to do with the spirituality of a homilist – a sensitive, even touchy matter among contemporaries. Here too the wisdom of the elders is safer, advice coming from St Augustine, Stephen Langton, Lacordaire and others. An extract from Vatican II's *Lumen Gentium* is also adduced. St Francis de Sales was the one to insist most strongly in his day that prayer was at the heart of the task of preaching. 'We should let fall the delicious honey of devotion,' he avers, 'drop by drop, now in the ear of one, now in the ear of another, praying secretly in your soul that God may let it sink into their hearts.'

I returned at the last to Daniel Francis, CSsR, and his insightful assertion about the pulpit being a mountain, with the preaching moment supplying what he calls 'the necessary experience of liminality, the "between-space" or threshold for the encounter with God'. Tennyson, Emily Dickinson and Sassoon, in that order, are recruited to homologate that crucial point.

Note
1.   Letter to *John Taylor*, 27 February 1818.

PART II

Sermons and Sermonettes

Some 'Occasional' Sermons

O most gentle pulpiter! What tedious homily of love you
have wearied your parishoners withal, and never cried:
'Have patience, good people'!
(Shakespeare, *As You Like It*, III, 2, 152)

The following preachments seem well to support the
theme of this book, varied as they are in style and time of
delivery. I have called them 'sermons' rather than
homilies, since my parish homilies have not been written
down and preserved, so what is offered here comes
within the category of 'occasional' preaching.

The first is based upon the words of Cardinal
Newman's *Lead, kindly light*, a poem which I came to
love in my time as a seminary student, and which I have
often used as a prayer since then. It provides much
pastoral nourishment besides food for private devotion.
The sermon was first given in King's College Chapel,
Aberdeen, at a morning service in 1990, and again, with
revisions, at an ecumenical occasion in Kinneff parish
church in 2005. The next sermon here included, for Lent,
was also given in King's College Chapel, in March 1990,
while I was working as Catholic Chaplain at the
University of Aberdeen.

The third sermon was first preached in the University
too, but has been kept in reserve for a while till given at
Canonmills Baptist church, Edinburgh. I have selected it

first of all because the book of Jonah, itself so droll, may benefit from literary support pointing up its more serious purposes; and secondly because folk respond with pleasure and interest to this superbly told story. This is followed by three further sermons delivered in Canonmills: a 'prologue' given on the eve of the world-famous Edinburgh International Festival, which each year hosts a feast of music and words; *Sing to the Lord a New Song*, preached at Eastertide, a time which cannot but inspire music and vocal expressions of Easter joy. The next, *The Raising of Lazarus*, is preoccupied with thoughts of death – death conquered by Christ – and the awakening to eternal joy in our heavenly homeland.

It is always a joy to be invited to associate with students and I was delighted to be asked some ten years ago to preach in the chapel of the University of St Andrews. It seemed appropriate to talk about the talents and gifts given to us by God and the use we make (or sadly, do not make) of them. Can we live up to God's expectations for us?

The final sermon included here became, as it were, an albatross around my neck for a time, though it has now slipped off and sunk quietly into the homiletic ocean. It was the piece offered for the *Preacher of the Year* event, sponsored jointly by the College of Preachers and *The Times*, the final of which took place in Southwark Anglican Cathedral in 1996. It is put forward here diffidently but, because it met with the approval of the adjudicating panel, and because it relies upon literature as a practical aid (apparently in tune with Professor Boyle's more lately discovered principles), I felt it must be included. The text is exactly that given on that tense and awesome occasion.

Lead, Kindly Light

The hymn we've just sung is arguably the most poetical piece in the hymn book. It can certainly stand on its own as a literary composition, with its sensitive imagery, its metrical delicacy and its secure rhythm. And the musical setting we've just enjoyed sets off the words very beautifully. Deeper than either of those, however, run John Henry Newman's *spiritual* insights.

The poet George Herbert, in lines entitled *A true hymn*, declares:

> The fineness which a hymn or psalm affords
> is when the soul unto the lines accords.

I find this opinion helpful when conventional ways of praying seem difficult or dry, when meditation becomes so misty, so patchy, as to obscure the normal route to prayerfulness. And then I'll open a hymn book, at times with system, at other times at random, and leaf through it slowly until somewhere my attention is arrested by a fine phrase, a powerful verse, a fresh inspiration; and the mist may start to clear, some concentration may return, and a renewed awareness of the presence of God comes on. I own that in certain of our modern hymnaries my searchings for illumination tend to be prolonged, the accord between the soul and the lines being rare! All a matter of taste, of course, one person's hymnological meat being another's hymnological poison! In any case, *Lead, kindly light* has for me much to offer by way of consolation and hope. Newman wrote it in 1833 on his return from a visit to Italy, when his ship was becalmed off Sicily, and he was anxious and troubled about many things.

Granted that the theme of the hymn is general, the *personal way* in which it is set is rather moving, much as our psalmist's was in our first lesson this morning, or as Psalm 139 is throughout in its one-to-one relationship between creature and creator. Here are a few verses from the latter psalm, in the seventeenth-century version by Mary Herbert, Countess of Pembroke:

> If forth I march, thou goest before
> If back I turn, thou com'st behind,
> So forth nor back
> Thy guard I lack,
> Nay on me too thy hand I find.
> Well I thy wisdom may adore,
> But never reach with earthy mind.

The notion of journeying, of pilgrimage, and a deep sense of God's unfailing protection – these are salient features too of our hymn.

There is no harm whatever, in our praying, if we choose to 'decorate' passages of prose or verse that we love, to 'festoon' them with ideas or imaginings that are useful to *us* as individuals. When we decorate a Christmas tree with lights and favours, we do so not to hide or deface the beauty of the tree but to build upon its inherent natural beauty. Similarly when we 'festoon' our prayers, we are only seeking for personal means of heightening our appreciation and enjoyment of the original. Perhaps among published work of this kind we may cite T. S. Eliot's lovely poems *The Journey of the Magi* and *A Song for Simeon*; and among practitioners of spiritual 'festooning' none other than C. S. Lewis was a self-acknowledged protagonist! So we are in good company!

Lead, kindly light serves as a not inappropriate overture to Lent, for the season makes sense only when we remember that its focus is the risen Christ, Light of the world, at Easter. We and all those who would follow him are, after all, a Paschal people, not only a Lenten one. On the other hand, the opportunities to come closer to our blessed Lord through a better understanding of and sharing in his suffering and Passion – such opportunities are myriad during the next few weeks. To use our hymn occasionally as an 'optional extra' may be a realistic and profitable exercise. Indeed it is a piece about travelling onward, reaching out towards eternity, but it's also about doubt and apparent failure, about darkness and shadows, about a total personal relationship with God. It is a prayer that Newman's work, that *all* our work, may come alive with vision and true hope.

'The night is dark, and I am far from home' is a line whose starkness will probably find a response in most folk's experience: from people like distant missionaries, students who are homesick, patients in hospital awaiting major surgery, or young persons hung up on alcohol or drugs. The prayer can't always be articulated, but the murkiness of night and the cry for love and understanding draw forth from countless human hearts a deep desire to emerge from the dark into daylight again. 'Lead thou me on' – strong, long monosyllables – by which the soul resigns itself to the inscrutable but tender mercies of the Almighty. And 'keep thou my feet', four more telling monosyllables, are words appealing for direction, for we know how wayward we may readily be, and how often we prefer the uncertain side roads, the perilous alleyways, to the path of righteousness and charity. But one step at a time is enough, free from undue anxiety about tomorrow, for the 'distant scene' – its place and its circumstances – are known to God alone. In a curious way we're apt to panic at the very length of Lent, to fret about our lasting it out, but if we are content to be pilgrims whose interest is each day and each day's march, serenity will be ours. And even though distant goals *are* clear in our minds, *pacing* ourselves is of the essence, as it is in so many areas of living, from sport itself to academic studies. So while we're entitled to think of the first verse of our hymn as a model of spiritual resignation, we have no right to imagine that this should be something passive. Its message is clear: 'lead thou me on' ... and on ... and I will strive to follow. Another hymn, an old favourite of mine, comes to mind here, with a parallel thought. It was written by St Thomas Aquinas, in Latin of course, and contains the prayer *per tuas semitas duc nos quo tendimus ad lucem quam inhabitas* – 'lead us by your paths in our forward progress to the light which you inhabit.'

I have heard *Lead, kindly light* described as the hymn of the 'three Rs', with the Resignation of Verse One leading into the Regret of Verse Two. Regret there undoubtedly is, with quite striking similarities of thought to Psalm 25's, but the admission 'I loved to choose and see my path' is instantly followed by 'but now, lead thou me on'. In other words, we have a sensible Christian approach here, combining sorrow for past shortcomings with a determination to allow God to take us over once again – what some of the older spiritual manuals would describe as 'a firm purpose of amendment'.

Newman talks of 'the garish day' he used to love and of his fears – remorse of conscience, presumably, about earlier times in his life. 'Garish' — the *mot juste*, surely, for it seems to convey the notion of a light that is other than kindly and inviting – artificial, rather, or dazzling, alluring almost. And the root of the trouble? Quite simply *pride*, we are told … Some of you (not all!) may remember the days in the Sixties especially, when gangs would daub walls with the information 'Tongs, or young Tollcross, or whatever, Rules O.K.'. Have *we* not all worn spiritual T-shirts of our own bearing the logo 'Pride rules O.K.'? 'Remember not past years' – an imperative cry from Newman, an imperative cry from the author of Psalm 25, an imperative cry from your heart and mine.

Of the 'three Rs', we've dealt first with Resignation and then with Regret. In the final verse I suggest we're dealing with Reliance. Put simply, Newman is acknowledging that God has looked after him so far, through thick and thin, and he trusts God will *never* let him down. He is *sure* his power 'will lead me on'. Or, as he expresses it in a different prayer: 'God does nothing in vain: he knows what he is about.' Then we come to that figurative phrase 'o'er moor and fen, o'er crag and torrent'. The kindly light will be there, certainly, but following it may not be easy. The moor may have to be climbed, with all its challenges and hazards. Possibly for years. Remember the words of Christina Rossetti:

> Does the road wind uphill all the way?
> Yes, to the very end.
> Will the day's journey take the whole long day?
> From morn to night, my friend.

The fen, on the other hand, may suggest those times when a person feels he or she is being sucked into a morass of trouble or depression from which escape seems remote, or when the marshy mists swirl around in distressful confusion. The crag may find us at a point in our journeying – at a moment of truth – say where sudden or painful decisions must be made, and we are terrified we may lose our balance, our foot may slip – and the gulf below looks menacing. And the torrent: allied maybe to the terror of the crag, the feeling is again one of being overwhelmed by turbulent forces from within or without, and of losing control the while. But through all this the light, the kindly light, will shine; the darkness will disperse in the end and the shadows flee. Childlike trust will be rewarded, however much and for however long we have been afraid, childlike, of the dark. Karl Rahner pitches the matter higher and in words appropriate to Lent when he says: 'Who knows whether a man may not be hanging at the right hand of the crucified on the scaffold of existence, if he accepts his destiny, silently and patiently, in ultimate fidelity to the light in the darkness?'

The conclusion of our hymn is at one with the spirit of yet another psalm, number 130: 'my soul is waiting for the Lord, more than watchman for daybreak: let the watchman *count* on daybreak, and Israel on the Lord.' And Newman's 'angel faces'? Oh, they must be dear ones who have reached the light before him. His yearning to be reunited with them is matched by personal longings of our own, till dawn comes and we all meet again. Newman's self-inscribed epitaph runs: *Ex umbra et imaginibus in veritatem* – 'out of the shade, away from appearances, into the truth'. He would have been in sympathy with this prayer which opens the liturgy of Ash

Wednesday: 'Father in heaven, the light of your truth bestows sight to the darkness of sinful eyes. May this season of repentance bring us the blessing of your forgiveness and the gift of your light. Amen.'

Lenten Thoughts

I would like to base our thoughts this morning upon two poems. Each fits easily into the requirements and atmosphere of Lent, and each owes its inspiration to the Gospel.

The first is a sonnet of the nineteenth century by Christina Rossetti. Its title is simply 'St Peter':

> St Peter once: 'Lord, dost thou wash my feet?' –
> Much more say I: Lord, dost thou stand and knock
> At my closed heart more rugged than a rock,
> Bolted and barred, for thy soft touch unmeet,
> Nor garnished, nor in any wise made sweet?
> Owls roost within and dancing satyrs mock.
> Lord, I have heard the crowing of the cock
> And have not wept: ah, Lord thou knowest it.
> Yet still I hear the knocking, still I hear:
> 'Open to Me, look on Me eye to eye,
> That I may wring thy heart and make it whole;
> And teach thee love because I hold thee dear,
> And sup with thee in gladness soul with soul,
> And sup with thee in glory by and by.'

The poem is a passionate one in its first eight lines; a wild piece of self-accusation and remorse, yet free from despair despite the fulsome expressions of regret. Indeed the author's awareness of the role of Peter in the Passion narrative provides her with a kind of parallel. Where he went wrong, she feels she has gone wrong. A sharer with him, no doubt, in the spirit of generous protestation: 'Lord, dost thou wash my feet?' she nevertheless realizes how weak and wayward her behaviour could become, how readily she could be trapped by the snares of temptation, as Peter was at the moment of his denials. Only the poem declares her guilt to be more heinous because her heart, she feels, was obdurate in a manner that Peter's was not: 'Lord, I have heard the crowing of the cock/And have not wept: ah, Lord, thou knowest it.' 'Ah, Lord, thou knowest it.' And with these words the theme takes an upward turn. It isn't yet repentance, it isn't yet confession – no, we're still rather in the realms of remorse – but it is an acknowledgement of the Lord's role in the problem, and that is enough to lead her into the second part of the dialogue, into the insistent response of Jesus to her unhappiness, a response of love, an individual response to her, beautifully at one with the way he dealt with the state and needs of particular persons in the Gospels. For Peter, when the cock crowed, a look was enough, for that made him go away and weep bitterly. But our poet, without losing anything in personal poignancy, carries Our Lord's reaction through to a promise not only of present reassurance but of future bliss. I wonder if the language of at least the first section doesn't remind you, as it does me, of the tone of some of John Donne's *Holy Sonnets*, while the outlook of the whole in some ways calls to mind the searchings of Francis Thompson in *The Hound of Heaven*

I don't think we are doing enough, however, simply by festooning the words of Christina Rossetti, by clarifying their import in terms of just the poet's emotions. At least, we're not doing enough if Lent is foremost in our thinking. Not that this season should make us introspective in any morbid or obsessional sense – that way lies the soul's malaise. But what the season can do is to lead us into a closer personal following of Christ through honest reappraisal. Two Lenten factors which are of importance to us all are these: first, a pledge that with God's help we want to strive seriously for a true 'change of heart'; secondly, that we do so by putting ourselves into his hands with childlike simplicity, all pretence and pretentiousness, all selfishness and self-importance cast resolutely aside.

So often people will ask us – do we not ask ourselves? – 'What shall I do for Lent?' And such requests, though well-intentioned, seem at times to miss the mark. The trouble lies perhaps in the idea many folk have that Lent is somehow not as it should be unless it's accompanied by this or that pious 'extra': giving up smoking, giving up sweets, giving up swearing, giving up the whole time, instead of concentrating on giving. Surplus enthusiasms have their place, of course, but Lent challenges us deep down, and there is no escape from its demands for that 'change of heart', the very same fundamental challenge that faced the author of Psalm 51 – this morning's first lesson – in his day. Sudden zeal in religious practice requires vigilance: otherwise we are no better than the patient who consumes a whole bottle of tummy tablets in one fell swoop, in the hope of achieving an instant cure. Let the zeal be soundly rooted first, and then we can add to it that sort of practice and penance that will supplement, not just ornament, the inner spiritual progress. Hair shirts of themselves will only wreak discomfort (warmer though they may be than many of the T-shirts one beholds around the campus). And they and any other forms of external mortification have no point unless they remind a person of the suffering and Passion and death of Christ, and lead to an intensification of our longing to serve him more and better.

Equally, no amount of giving Lenten alms to the Third World or anyone else can be of benefit to our souls if it is merely a kind of conscience money, and not a gift of love to our needy brothers and sisters in Christ, and done in his name and for his sake: 'Create in me a clean heart, O God, and put a new and right spirit within me.'

The second poem I'd like to offer you is an anonymous work from the seventeenth century. It deals fancifully yet vividly with an incident recorded in the Gospel of St Luke (Chapter 23): Our Lord's sublime forgiveness of him whom tradition calls 'the good thief':

> Say bold but blessed thief
> That in a trice
> Slipped into paradise,
> And in plain day
> Stol'st heaven away,
> What trick couldst thou invent
> To compass thy intent?
> What arms?
> What charms?
> 'Love and belief.'
>
> Say bold but blessed thief,
> How couldst thou read
> A crown upon that head?
> What text, what gloss,
> A kingdom on a cross?
> How couldst thou come to spy
> God in a man to die?
> What light?
> What sight?
> 'The sight of grief –

I sight to God his pain;
And by that sight
I saw the light;
Thus did my grief
Beget relief.
And take this rule from me,
Pity thou him, he'll pity thee.
Use this,
Ne'er miss,
Heaven may be stol'n again.'

You will remember the Gospel's words: 'And he said: "Jesus, remember me when you come in your kingly power." And he said to him: "Truly, I say to you: today you will be with me in Paradise."'

It's a graphic cameo, and it's profoundly moving. I always link it with a woodcarving of the crucifixion I saw in reproduction years ago, where the head of Christ, crowned with thorns and blood-bespattered, had about it a dignity and compassion in the midst of agony that caught the noble simplicity of St Luke's account perfectly. The poem's language cleverly plays with the notion of theft throughout: 'slipped into paradise ... stol'st heaven away ... heaven may be stol'n again.'

To the question 'How did you do it?' the thief replies quite simply, 'Love and belief.' And to the question 'How could you recognize God upon the cross beside you?' his answer is that it was the sight of grief. And both questions are put, if not cynically, then with more than a hint that the thief had used cunning means to acquire his reward. But both answers are totally direct and disarming. Indeed, our blessed Lord is reacting even here, amid the torture and humiliation of crucifixion, with his characteristic blend of directness and grace that abounds in the pages of the Gospels. 'Your faith has made you whole' is as usual underlying his reaction, his immediate reaction, to a repentant sinner. Only this time, because time is short, there is no need to add: 'Go and sin no more.' This time, time and eternity are nearly at one. And while the whole episode amazes us, for the infinite mercy of Jesus ever leaves us that way, it must go further. It must inspire us to try to be less unworthy, to seek actively after (may I say it again?) a Lenten change of heart.

In the Lord's Prayer, said by us so often, but how often really prayed, are the words: 'Forgive us our trespasses, as we forgive those who trespass against us.' The dependency of the first upon the second part is emphasized, for in St Matthew's Gospel Our Lord goes on: 'If you forgive men their trespasses, your heavenly Father also will forgive you; but if you do not forgive men their trespasses, neither will your Father forgive your trespasses.'

Every one of us knows how hard it is to live up to this. We can be quite impossible – now liverish, now volatile, now moody, in no way disposed to Christian generosity, to dispensing unilateral pardons. Yet what a nerve we have to expect the other party to a quarrel, the other sharer in a misunderstanding, to do all the apologizing, or even as we'd sometimes have it, all the grovelling. Oh, we may feign surprise sometimes at the way other people behave in this regard, until we realize what a plank is affecting our view of ourselves.

So we'll leave aside others with family feuds, for example, which forbid folk to talk to each other at weddings or funerals, or lead to litigation over the inheriting of a tea set. I will only draw back a personal veil for an instant to tell you, now that it's over, what years it took me to forgive my school mathematics teacher. His failing to make me numerate was due more to my crassness than to his teaching inadequacy. But the nub of my resentment lay elsewhere. You see, one day he took my packed lunch out of my desk, hit me over the head with it, and sent me outside to feed the seagulls. They were duly grateful, but my wrath was insatiable, and the fact that the rest of the class had tittered added salt to the wound. And for ages I nursed that wrath, to keep it warm. But that kind of brooding over an injury, even in a youngster, is clean contrary to imitating Christ. And what a moment of grace it is to discover the point of forgiveness, to move away from a ludicrous sense of disappointment that the other party was not really to blame, and from the fondling and fostering of an old injury. And this can be quite as important when the wrong resides more in the imagination than in reality.

Our battle lies sometimes in overcoming that animal sense of the hostile which lies somewhere under the surface for most of us, and has fear as its nourisher. It lies too within the human propensity for revenge, something primitive or unholy if you will, but latent and readily aroused if we are careless. It lies again within the sphere of what we may choose to call justice, only the justice that banishes forgiveness is alien to mercy, and dallies with cruelty and heartlessness. And the agony of the person awaiting forgiveness is increased.

We cannot enjoy the fruits of salvation, then, without contributing towards salvation through Christ-like love of our neighbour. God is the real and primary pardoner, and each man and woman is his child. Our powers of forgiveness are derived from his. St Peter and the good thief encountered the Saviour and his goodness personally, and their response to that goodness and mercy may serve us as a special inspiration throughout this Lenten season.

'Second Thoughts' –
Reflections on the Book of Jonah

Recently some of the poems of Emily Dickinson have come my way. She spent a self-effacing life in Massachusetts, and created a considerable corpus of poetry, discovered only after her death in 1886. One piece, typically brief and whimsical, is about 'second thoughts', my subject this morning, and I'd like to use it as an introduction:

> A Thought went up my mind today –
> That I have had before –
> But did not finish – some way back –
> I could not fix the Year –
> Nor where it went – nor why it came
> The second time to me –
> Nor definitely, what it was –
> Have I the art to say –
> But somewhere – in my Soul – I know –
> I've met the Thing before –
> It just reminded me – 'twas all –
> And came my way no more –

Such a quotation might well have been used by a classics master I once had who loved all manner of literary gems. One that he'd visit upon some pupil extricating himself from any hideous solecism was derived from Euripides: 'second thoughts somehow are wiser!'

A like notion may spring to mind when we look at the third chapter of the Book of Jonah, a work of uncertain date and authorship that holds within a brief compass a wealth of lively narrative, insight into human behaviour, moral reflection and even humour. Yes, humour; for we cannot but smile over the episode of the prophet's residency in the belly of the whale, or at his sulking in the shade of the eucalyptus plant which God then summarily withers. A beguiling irony (alien to the writing of history) pervades the story, and the Scottish playwright James Bridie alighted upon this in his comedy *Jonah and the Whale*. The latter is portrayed in gentlemanly fashion, as, for instance, when he enquires of the prophet: 'for three days and three nights, out of consideration for your situation, I have had nothing to drink. Would you mind very, very much if I shipped a few gallons? Can you swim?'

Our present interest focuses upon the occasion of Jonah's emerging from the fish upon dry land, his first attempt to flee from the Lord's presence having been spectacularly thwarted. *Now* the tone sounds more urgent, more peremptory than before. Jonah is ordered again to get up and go to Nineveh, 'that great city', and to upbraid and challenge its people for their unspecified evil. In a delicious hyperbole, Nineveh is suddenly described as being 'three days' journey in breadth'. Quite how Jonah felt about his daunting task we are not told. The point is that, upon God's second insistence, *he did go and he did* deliver his message. The nub of his stern tidings was: 'Yet forty days, and Nineveh shall be overthrown.' The consequence was that not only the entire citizenry but also the king himself repented in sackcloth and ashes. A startling conversion! A single brief oracle, and all (including, apparently, the animals) had an improving change of heart. One scholar wryly describes the Ninevites as 'uncommonly repentant Gentiles'!

At any rate, we find here the fruits of 'second thoughts' not only in the prophet, over-persuaded by God to undertake his mission afresh, but also among the populace whose reaction was practically instantaneous. It's when we begin to tease out from the whole Book lessons for ourselves that we may become slightly unnerved. Take Jonah himself to start with: there's probably something of his character in all of us. We may at times be unaware, totally, of the call to do God's bidding in correcting someone we *know* to have done a rash or wicked thing. St Augustine, in his sermon on the Shepherds, quotes these words of the Lord given through the prophet Ezekiel:

> If you do not speak to warn the wicked to turn from his way, that wicked man shall die in his iniquity, but his blood I will require at your hand. But if you warn the wicked to turn from his way, and he does not turn from his way, he shall die in his iniquity, but you will have saved your life (3:18–19).

Our conscience cries out in the name of justice or charity, but we discover a way out – a winking with one eye or a closing of both – arising from human respect or some other aspect of cowardice. As the American poet Thomas John Carlisle put it:

> The word came
> and he went
> in the other
> direction.
> God said: Cry
> tears of compassion
> tears of repentance;
> cry against
> the reek
> of unrighteousness;
> cry for

the right turn
the contrite spirit.
And Jonah rose
and fled
in tearless
silence.

So often we want, like Jonah at first, to flee the Lord's presence 'in tearless silence' and hide. What gives us the right to sit in judgement? Am I my brother's keeper? Strange, isn't it, how slow we are to work for another's amendment when we should, yet how swift to criticize the offender behind his back when we most certainly shouldn't? We rush towards unkind conclusions about others whilst pretending there is no beam, no plank in our own eye. Poor Jonah, whose fatuous conduct in running away from God we smirkingly condemn, failing the while to recognize in his actions so much that typifies our own! The telling words of Robert Burns (in his poem *To a Louse*) are fully apposite:

O wad some pow'r the giftie gie us
To see oursels as others see us!
It wad frae mony a blunder free us,
And foolish notion.

And so we turn again to the people of Nineveh and their king. Their second thoughts had come speedily, for they were terrified by those ominous words: 'yet forty days, and Nineveh shall be overthrown.' Surely the commentator who sees in this Book 'a change in the prophet's role from a deliverer of oracles to a *persuader*' is being unduly bland. Blandness, however, is not a feature of scriptural academics, particularly within their own household!

The administering of a short, sharp shock frequently achieves its objective! Mercifully the days of corporal punishment in schools are over, though the older among us may recall how a recalcitrant pupil might be made remorseful by a single swish! (To say he had 'second thoughts' would over-intellectualize the experience!) Even in spiritual matters a quick rebuke may have its place to restore the wayward soul to righteousness. Elderly clergy will not have been immune. A fellow-student of mine, in ancient days, now a Bishop, was mortified to be told publicly in the refectory (by the sharp-tongued Vice-Rector) to 'stop sniggering like a half-baked schoolgirl'. And I have it on unimpeachable authority how a young novice was reading aloud in the convent refectory something about music. 'Beethoven,' she said, 'Mozart and *Bach*', pronounced 'batch'. 'Bach, Sister,' interrupted the English Mother-Superior, 'Bach.' So the hapless novice responded shyly: 'Woof-woof, Mother!'

Any animadversions, to be effective, should not offend. The fiery Paul himself would have none of that. No, even if the correction is trenchant it must have charitable intent, hence benefiting both the deliverer and the recipient. Otherwise there will be fear on the one side, arrogance on the other.

Jonah and the people of Nineveh each had second thoughts. But what about God? The text runs thus: 'And God saw their works, that they turned from their evil way, and God repented of the evil that he said he would do unto them, and he did it not.'

What an insight into the mercy of the Almighty! Indeed the author highlights a special quality of it: it is free and unmerited, and generously bestowed upon any contrite soul. This concept is famously expressed through Shakespeare by Portia in *The Merchant of Venice*:

> The quality of mercy is not strained . . .
> It is an attribute to God himself,
> And earthly power doth then show likest God's
> When mercy seasons justice.

There is happily no room for doubt. God's compassion towards the repentant sinner is and always has been gracious, for the Ninevites as portrayed in our story, and for us. May he grant us now and at the end a humble, contrite heart, and may our New Testament awareness of Christ's mercy uphold our confidence as we return to Emily Dickinson with this lovely gloss on St Matthew's twenty-fifth chapter, the parable of the sheep and the goats. It's in dialogue form:

> 'Unto *me*?' I do not know you –
> Where may be your house?
>
> 'I am Jesus, late of Judea –
> Now – of Paradise.'
>
> Wagons have you to convey me?
> *This* is far from *thence* –
>
> 'Arms of mine – sufficient phaeton –
> Trust omnipotence.'
>
> I am spotted – 'I am pardon':
> I am small – 'The least
> Is esteemed in Heaven the Chiefest –
> Occupy my house.'

Fellowship and Harmony

All nations, clap your hands;
shout with a voice of joy to God. *(Psalm 47)*

When it comes to music, literature, or art, much depends on our earliest experiences. My own interest in music and drama was largely due to a dear, eccentric friend who produced the plays at George Watson's, and who had no mean appreciation of art and also music. He would take me, and other pupils he knew, to all sorts of plays and concerts, and opened up for us more and more vistas of cultural joy. As for art, I'd drop into the galleries at the foot of the Mound from time to time, often with my mother, whose favourite paintings often became mine too.

I never had boyhood dreams of becoming an engine driver. I did, however, toy with the idea of being a vet, or, if not a vet, at least an actor. The first notion was scotched by my realistic science teacher, and I saw later that it was perfectly possible to love all creatures great and small without actually being a vet.

The other idea was firmly discouraged by a priest who'd once been a professional actor, Fr Eric Barber, who felt I was *far* too tender a plant to survive the hurly-burly of a stage career. So I've always been one of the audience, contentedly. The King's and Lyceum theatres, the Assembly Hall, the Gateway in its time, along with the Usher Hall and the other concert venues, were places of stimulus and enjoyment.

I was sixteen when the first Edinburgh Festival took place. What a venture, what an adventure it was. With the blessing of the city fathers, and under the powerful direction of Rudolf Bing, Edinburgh burst upon the wider cultural arena in a spirit of visionary zeal. The excited expectation of so much post-war activity was still in the air. This city had taken up a mighty challenge which doubters may have looked on as madness; but the bow had been drawn at a venture, and the arrow would fly far and true. The Festival is still with us, replete with vigour and flair, though the Fringe may occasionally seem to have lost a little of its youthful idealism. Yet one event, rock-like and constant, its glorious setting unalterable, the Military Tattoo, remains triumphant.

I hope I'm not slipping into that mindset described by the Roman poet Horace: 'testy, a grumbler inclined to praise the way the world went when *he* was a boy, to play the critic and censor of the new generation. The tide of years,' he goes on, 'the tide of years, as it rises, brings many advantages; as it ebbs, carries many away.' Yet I do hold that some of the early Festivals stood out: few conductors, from however far afield, have bettered that doughty quartet of British maestros, Beecham, Boult, Sargent and Barbirolli; the *Three Estates* has been the finest thing presented in the Assembly Hall, and Verdi's *Requiem*, with the Milan Orchestra and Chorus under Victor de Sabata, took its audiences to the very portals of heaven. As for the Fringe, drama reached the heights with *The Strong are Lonely*, with Donald Wolfit, no less, and *The Playboy of the Western World* with Siobhan McKenna, or the stage version of *The Ebb Tide* by our own Robert Louis Stevenson. Opera too, with those first Glyndebourne Productions, was world class from the start – Verdi, Rossini, Mozart, etc. Exhibitions of great art have graced most Festivals too.

Now there's something amiss, for so far there's been just one mention of God. J. S. Bach held that music should be made for the glory of God and the re-creation of mankind, and numbers of writers have had deep insights into music's spiritual qualities. Take Shakespeare in *The Merchant of Venice*:

> The man that hath no music in himself
> nor is not moved with concord of sweet sounds
> is fit for treasons, stratagems and spoils;
> The motions of his spirit are dull as night
> and his affections dark as Erebus;
> let no such man be trusted.

And here's what John Dryden says near the beginning of his *Ode for St Cecilia's Day*:

> From harmony, from heavenly harmony
> the universal frame began
> from harmony to harmony
> through all the compass of the notes it ran,
> the diapason closing full in man

(A diapason apparently refers to the whole compass and range of organ notes.)

What a lovely image that is of God's creation of the world, referred to by Henry Vaughan as 'the gret chima and symphony of Nature'. It's as if we might dare to think that, instead of 'God saw that it was good', the Book of Genesis might equally well have said, 'God saw that it was harmonic'. After all, harmony is derived from the Greek word meaning the fitting-together-of-things, or, if you prefer, the work of art of a carpenter. You can say artificer or architect, but the concept is the same. Linked to that, listen to these few lines of Wordsworth from *The Prelude*, where some of our terminology occurs:

> Dust as we are, the immortal spirit grows
> Like harmony in music; there is a dark
> Inscrutable workmanship that reconciles
> Discordant elements, makes them cling together
> In one society.

God, who is love, would have us love him wholeheartedly, and our neighbour as ourselves for his sake. In other words, the God of all harmony wants his children to be philharmonic too. Order, harmony, love should be the mark of his followers; not chaos, enmity and discord. There are even hints of this insight among the early pagan thinkers. Plato, for instance, referred to 'love, harmony, in whose footsteps everyone ought to follow, celebrating him excellently in song, and bearing each his part in that divinest harmony which Love sings to all things which live and are, soothing the troubled minds of gods and men.'

Yet, ever since the fall of Adam mankind has opted again and again for the forbidden fruit or, in New Testament terms, has preferred darkness to light. Truly the Word was made flesh and dwelt among us, truly he was the perfect model of self-giving love, and he longs for us to follow his example. However, down the centuries, and into our own day, folk have hardened their hearts and have not listened to his voice. Endowed with free will, people have been attracted to evil – everything from personal sins to genocide and international terrorism, those woeful scourges of our time.

May we now refocus our thoughts, prayerfully, on the

Edinburgh Festival, and where the old psalmist says 'Jerusalem', shall we *think* Edinburgh? 'Jerusalem is built as a city, strongly compact; it is there that the tribes go up, the tribes of the Lord ... For the peace of Jerusalem pray: peace be to your homes. May peace reign in your walls, in your palaces peace.'

The Festival's artistic thrust, to be valuable and valid, must promote and foster harmony, bound up, as we've seen, with brotherly and sisterly love. But turn that idea on its head for a moment. Imagine you're enjoying a concert, when all of a sudden one member of the orchestra, anything from the piccolo to the double-bass, decides to ignore the composer and conductor, and proceeds to play something apart from the score, with Mr Bean-like abandon. Disaster!

Or suppose an actor, asserting his individuality, sidesteps the script in favour of some personal tirade, there'd be an outcry, not least from the prompt corner. Pursue the image, and think of God as humanity's director or conductor, having for each of his children a particular life to be led, a unique path to follow.

Listen to R. S. Thomas's inspiring poem, *The Conductor*:

> Finally at the end of the day,
> When the sun was buried and
> There was no more to say,
> He would lift idly his hand,
> And softly the small stars'
> Orchestra would begin
> Playing over the first bars
> Of the night's overture.
> He listened with the day's breath
> Bated, trying to be sure

That what he heard was at one
With his own score, that nothing,
No casual improvisation
Or sounding of a false chord,
Troubled the deep peace.
It was this way he adored
With a god's ignorance of sin
The self he had composed.

Our objective should therefore be clear. If we want to play in God's orchestra, however humbly – maybe just with a touch on the triangle at the proper time – and if we want to play a part in the drama in which he has cast us – even if it seems to be an unremarkable walk-on role – then harmony must be the watchword.

Return with me to some youthful artistic experience: if you ever played in a school orchestra or acted in a school play, was it just to show off? Of course not; you did it as a member of a team. Oh it was fun, it was fulfilling, yes, but above all it was for the good of the community. Our friend Dryden, in the poem mentioned earlier, so sublimates artistic achievement as to state that, when the organ was invented, 'An angel heard, and straight appeared, /Mistaking earth for heaven.' Still, one sometimes wonders how an angel *could* feel at home in this discordant world of today.

But courage: We are not in the slough of Despond; for, despite many periods of turbulence and strife, Edinburgh has long played its part, and still does, in fostering the Arts, wherein many of her sons and daughters have excelled, some far furth of Scotland. We thank God for them and for their gifts. And in this, the Festival's sixtieth year, may we hope for a renewal of that spirit of harmony that marked the early years.

We have then a lovely amalgam of hope and thanksgiving as we anticipate three weeks of fellowship and harmony. And who can tell where that harmony may make its home in this Mozartian season? Perhaps in the comforted heart of some visitor from a far-off land, or perhaps in ours. 'Oh, let all the world, in every corner sing: my God and King!'

'Sing to the Lord a New Song!'

Words and music will occupy our thoughts for a little while this morning, and they'll clearly have an Easter connection. By way of an overture, I'd like to begin with a few lovely lines from the poet John Donne, writing here not directly about Easter, but imagining himself to be in preparation to join, in due course, those who make music for ever in heaven in gladsome praise. He writes:

> Since I am coming to that holy room,
> Where, with thy choir of saints for evermore,
> I shall be made thy music; as I come
> I tune the instrument here at the door,
> And what I must do then, think here before.

So, in faith and hope, and within a kind of family orchestra, we tune *our* instruments and raise *our* voices in honour of him who came down from heaven for the world's salvation, and who rose from the dead on the third day in accordance with the Scriptures. Oh, our whole earthly lives may be but an overture, a prelude, but Our Lord has promised a share in his glorious resurrection to those who have loved him in this life, and who have striven, according to their lights, to walk in his ways.

God has, as it were, provided us with the score. It is up to us to get on with practising our scales assiduously every day, and prayerfully, with something of the anticipation John Donne has outlined in his verses.

When you and I last met to worship together, it was at the start of the 2006 Edinburgh International Festival.

You may recall some of the wonderful music we enjoyed, both vocal and instrumental, including the Halleluiah Chorus whose theme we'll return to anon. Allow me, then, with music in mind, to link that occasion and this with a few lines of George Herbert, from his poem entitled *Easter*:

> Awake, my lute, and struggle for thy part
> With all thy art.
> The cross taught all wood to resound his name,
> Who bore the same.
> His stretched sinews taught all strings, what key
> Is best to celebrate this most high day.

For a text from Scripture, let's go to Hebrew poetry to find these words of Psalm 149, so often quoted in church during the Easter season: 'sing to the Lord a new song, his praise in the assembly of the faithful.' Our ancient Israelite's bidding is echoed in mood and purpose on this greatest of all Christian festivals ... Yet, when it comes to expressing our joy in cathedral, church or chapel, we find that we're inclined to restrain our zeal. We may be a shade diffident about letting ourselves go within hallowed surroundings. Douce citizens of Edinburgh, or Aberdeen, for that matter, we don't think it is quite the thing to do. I can imagine my late granny declaring from her Colinton bungalow: 'It's just a little vulgar, dear.' Mind you, all styles of church service merit respect, but the truth of Easter and its glorious tidings *demand* that we be joyful, that we should be merrier even than at Christmas. Indeed the prescribed liturgy (of those who follow such) insists on a close involvement for everyone, say at the Easter Vigil, with its symbolic lighting of the new fire, the veneration of the Paschal candle (symbol of Christ, Light of the world), and the blessing of the freshly filled font, in which the newest candidates will receive baptism. I am very aware, by the way, that participation here is intense and purposeful from Palm Sunday right through to Easter itself.

St Augustine, that learned churchman of the fifth century, has some stimulating thoughts for us to ponder. Never mind that some folk have found him tedious, or consider his sermons interminable, for some of his reflections on Easter are both brief and stimulating. He points out how the new song quoted at the start from our psalmist is a thing of gladness and love. Then, moving the lines into a Christian context, he declares: 'The man who has learned to live a new life has learned to sing a new song.' 'For a new man,' he continues, 'a new song and the New Testament all belong to the same kingdom.' So the new man or woman will sing a new song, and belong to the New Testament. Yes, at this season, in church or out of it we want to celebrate and to sing. 'This is the day which the Lord has made, let us rejoice and be glad therein' – these words are as fitting today, the octave of Easter, as they were last Sunday. Indeed they befit the whole period of Eastertide, seven weeks in all.

So, this triumphant holiday of ours cannot but inspire music and produce singing, as our hearts' happiness in the Resurrection spills over into vocal expressions of joy. But St Augustine won't allow us to stop there, for he goes on 'You sing, of course you sing, I can hear you; but make sure your life sings the same tune as your mouth.' Then picking up the psalmist's words, 'his praise in the assembly of the faithful', he adds, thought-provokingly, 'The singer himself is the praise contained in the song.'

The singer himself is the praise contained in the song. In other words, if we want to vocalize the praise of God, we must ourselves *be* what we speak or sing. So it looks as if the singing of Easter hymns, though admirable and proper, will scarcely do on its own. Would greater attention to the words solve the problem? Psalm 45 begins confidently: 'My heart is stirred by a noble theme . . . my tongue is the pen of an expert scribe.' Well, wait! St Augustine doesn't seem to think that *is* the solution. He focuses his attention rather on the music as music. 'Sing to God,' he commands, 'but not out of tune! Will you ever command an art so polished that you need know no fear of jarring on that perfect listener's ear, God's ear?'

So we are not to search primarily for words, for of themselves they simply cannot express what we're singing in our hearts. 'At the harvest or in the vineyard,' says our saint, 'whenever men must labour hard, they *begin* to celebrate with *words* that manifest their joy; but when their joy brims over, they give themselves over to the sheer sound of singing . . . And to whom does this jubilation most belong? Surely to God, who is unutterable. So, if words will not come and you may not remain silent, what else can you do but let the melody soar?' Maybe, after all, there's spiritual merit for those of us who, in the exuberance of cleansing, 'lah-lah' sacred music in the bath: Walter Savage Landor, in lines to Robert Browning, states consolingly: 'There is delight in singing, though none hear beside the singer.'

Still, there is possibly a word we can use, or at least a Paschal utterance going by the name of a word – more a yell of praise than anything. It's 'Alleluia!'

It occurs frequently in the final fifty psalms, and once each in the books of Tobit and Revelation respectively.

The Early Church retained the word in its original Hebrew form, Halleluiah: 'Praise the Lord'; and we know from St Jerome that little ones were taught to articulate it almost as soon as they could speak; and it was sung during his, Jerome's, lifetime by the country folk of Palestine while they drove the plough. For our part, we can say it or sing it on our own throughout Eastertide, or recite it congregationally in church; and we push the expression to the limits and beyond, realizing that not only our tongues and our voices should praise God, but also our conscience, thoughts and deeds. Collectively and individually, the psalms are on our side, with on the one hand our special text, 'his praise in the assembly of the faithful', and on the other, Psalm 103's 'Bless the Lord, oh my soul, and let all that is within me bless his holy name.'

We are glorifying God this morning gathered together prayerfully in this place, this bonded fellowship in Canonmills. Excellent; and there is no room for any corollary that our praise will or should diminish when we leave to go home. The prospect of Sunday lunch should engender more thanksgiving, not less: How silly it would be to cast off our gladness at the church portal, and replace it with gloomy looks. In sum, provided we don't stop trying to live a good life, and don't stop wanting to serve Christ in all we say, and think, and do, we will be *praising* God continually. St Augustine puts it beautifully: 'If you never turn aside from a holy life, though your tongue is silent, your life speaks loud. God has ears for what your heart is saying. For just as we have ears for men's voices, God has ears for their thoughts.'

The season recently completed, named Lent (from Middle English, we're told), is an anticipatory word –

meaning Spring. It is a happy fact that, in our land, Easter
and Springtime coincide. Indeed, that lovely sign of
Spring, the daffodil, is sometimes called the Lent lily. The
natural harmonizes, as it were, with the supernatural.
Earth seems to be attuned to our spiritual mood of renewal
and exhilaration. This view is sustained by the poet Gerard
Manley Hopkins in an early work called *Easter*. Part of it
runs thus – oh, and see if you can't detect something of
Keats in it, or even a Shakespeare song:

> Gather gladness from the skies;
> Take a lesson from the ground; Flowers do ope
> their heavenward eyes
> And a springtime joy hath found,
> Earth throws winter's robes away;
> Decks herself for Easter day.

And Francis Thompson, in a passage on exactly the same
theme, offers this delicious notion: 'Let even the slug-
abed snail upon the thorn/ Put forth a conscious horn!'
Alleluia!

The Raising of Lazarus

As for me, in my justice I shall see your face, and
be filled, when I awake, with the sight of your glory.

(Psalm 17)

I'd like to continue with lines written by that seventeenth-
century genius, John Donne, in which he vigorously
defies death:

Death, be not proud, though some have called thee
Mighty and dreadful, for thou art not so;
For those whom thou thinkest thou dost over throw
Die not, poor Death, nor yet canst thou kill me.
From rest and sleep, which but thy pictures be,
Much pleasure – then, from thee much more must flow;
And soonest our best men with thee doth go,
Rest of their bones and soul's delivery.
Thou'rt slave to fate, chance, kings, and desperate men,
And dost with poison, war and sickness dwell;
And poppy or charms can make us sleep as well,
And better than thy stroke. Why swellst thou then?
One short sleep past, we wake eternally,
And death shall be no more. Death, thou shalt die.

Ah, one short sleep past, we wake eternally . . . Balance
that with the Psalmist's 'and be filled, when I awake,
with the sight of your glory'.

Can you remember the first time you heard or read the
account of the raising of Lazarus; or the first time it made
an impact? I can. It was in the Lyceum Theatre, here in
Edinburgh, more than sixty years ago, in a production of
Dostoevsky's *Crime and Punishment*. The cast included

John Gielgud and Edith Evans; but it was a young actress called Audrey Fildes who read out the Lazarus passage to the play's most disturbed character. I was very moved by it, and it has moved me ever since. It deals remarkably with matters of life and death, and of the involvement of Jesus in both. Today we are reminded that the raising of Lazarus embraces the claim: Jesus is the life whom we are seeking.

Though death is an inevitable factor in human existence, the Christian consolation resides in this truth: that although death is inevitable, it is not the end. Christ the Lord has power over sin and death, over *life and death*; and we, if we are faithful to him, will not encounter death for ever, but have a share in his glorious resurrection. This sharing he has promised to those who have loved him in this life and striven to follow his ways. The story of the raising of Lazarus is overwhelmingly powerful, and personally reassuring to us all. It gives us besides lovely insights into the humanity of Jesus, leave alone for the moment the subsequent miracle.

As Man, Jesus was upset, distressed over the death of his friend; he sighed and wept over it, 'with a sigh that came straight from the heart'. Writing in the eleventh century, one Theophylact said: 'To prove his human nature he sometimes gives it free vent, while at other times he commands and restrains it by power of the Holy Spirit. Our Lord,' he continues,

> allows his nature to be affected in these ways, both to prove that he is very Man, not Man in appearance only; and also to teach us by his own example the due measures of joy and grief. For the absence altogether of sympathy and sorrow is brutal, the excess of them weakly.

There's another human touch, a curious one, in his apparent reluctance to respond at once to Martha's message that Lazarus, his friend, was ill. He took his time (possibly to test the sister's faith), though his response was, as it always was, one of courtesy and patience.

When Jesus did arrive at Bethany, Martha showed that indeed her faith *was* strong – stronger at this point than that of the disciples – and was rewarded with one of the most forceful of Our Lord's statements recorded in the Gospels: 'I am the Resurrection and the Life', followed by the assurance that the one who believes in him will never die. Wherever 'life' is mentioned in this Gospel of John, it signifies the life of the Father and the Son that is shared by the believer. 'Do you believe this?' he says to us today, 'Do *you* believe this?' Belief in him – in who he is, in what he said, and in his triumph over death itself – that is the very core of our faith.

Imagine the tension by the tomb: what would Jesus do? What could he do? Commenting on Jesus' command, 'Take the stone away', the fourth-century scholar St John Chrysostom asks: 'But why did he not raise Lazarus without taking away the stone? Could not he who moved a dead body by his voice, much more have moved a stone?' 'He purposely did not do so,' says Chrysostom, 'in order that the miracle might take place in the sight of all; to give no room for saying, as they had said in the case of the blind man (ch. 9), This is not he. *Now* they might go into the grave, and feel and see that Lazarus *was* the man.'

Lazarus's illness is inextricably connected with a manifestation of God's glory. God's power shines out though Jesus' sign.

It is interesting to speculate about Lazarus and his state of consciousness. We don't know, and we never can know, what his experience must have been during those few days in which he was dead. We wonder what he may have seen and felt, how far into God's presence he may have come within that time; and we can only imagine his stupefaction upon hearing from the dead the cry of his friend from outside the tomb, 'Lazarus, come forth!' And come forth he did.

Now you would have thought, would you not, that all those who were standing about, not just some, or even those who had merely heard of those events, would have doubted no longer about the identity of Jesus or, at least, would have been so overcome, so awestruck, as never in the future to offer him any sort of harm. It is clear from the final sentence of our passage that the faith of some prompted continuous witness. And yet, within a very short time, so many of his own people, among whom he had come as the Word made flesh, rejected him totally, barbarously, mockingly, sending him to a death of excruciating pain on Calvary, that green hill far away.

When we think of it – dare we think of it? – about all we have been given, all we have been told, indeed all we know about our blessed Lord, we blush to think how easily and how often *we* have been, if not at the centre, at least, through sin, on the verges, of those who said then to Christ, and still say, 'No', and who in effect would reject him again.

When a person dies, that person does not complete his or her existence because, for the dead, life is changed, not ended. When the remains of our earthly bodies lie in death, we gain an everlasting dwelling-place in heaven. The one who dies enters into an entirely new dimension of life, of which Lazarus for a little while had a foretaste. Oh, there is always at a funeral in church or crematorium, a great division within our hearts, one part insisting that our humanity, like our Lord's momentarily, give way to sorrow and tears, the other part, deeper down and stronger still, holding to that faith assuring us, in our fellowship with Christ, that we will never pass into oblivion; assuring us also that the deceased will reap the reward of eternal life; and assuring us further that we shall see him or her again and enjoy their company everlastingly in the presence of God.

Let the words from today's Gospel passage that have rung down the centuries and inspired so many before us, inspire us too this day. Christ, who raised Jairus's daughter from the dead, and raised from the dead the son of the widow of Naim, and who raised Lazarus, and raised *himself* from the dead, will never let go of our hands, never allow us to be lost or encounter anything other than heaven, provided we pursue a faithful pilgrimage, hold to the truths that matter most, and put ourselves lovingly into the hands of God and of his Son, Jesus Christ.

I earlier gave a personal reminiscence. Please allow me another. Some years ago, I was a member of the chaplaincy team in Aberdeen Royal Infirmary. One Saturday, I'd just come home from a wedding, when I was called to a patient with serious heart trouble in Intensive Care. Having squeezed my way past all the equipment, and in my haste put on the ward gown back to front, I said some prayers, read a little Scripture, gave him a blessing and departed. Here is one of the prayers I used:

God of compassion,
our human weakness lays claim to your strength.
We pray that through the skills of surgeons and nurses,
your healing gifts may be granted to this patient.
May your servant respond to your healing will
and be re-united with us at your altar of praise.
Grant this through Christ our Lord.

A couple of days later, the Sister of that ward ran after
me to say that the surgeon, a gracious, unassuming
Indian, would like a word. He told me that they had been
keeping that patient artificially alive till I arrived. 'I don't
know what you did,' he said, 'but, soon after you went
away, normal functioning was restored to Mr X, and in a
few days we'll be sending him back to Dundee to
recuperate. And by the way,' he added, 'I've decided to
call him from now on my Lazarus patient.' I, of course,
had done nothing. The friend of the risen Lazarus
manifestly had. 'Death, thou shalt die': thus John Donne,
and thus we also, arising from a total trust in Him who
first said: 'I am the Resurrection and the Life.'

A Use of Gifts[1]

Any University – and this one no less than others – is full of gifted people. And the gifts are evident in so many fields of academic study that any unfamiliar observer would be amazed: from Science to History, English to Divinity, Law to Modern Languages, the range is huge, the disciplines extraordinarily varied. To all this may be added the subsidiary gifts displayed in the undergraduate sphere by students with zeal, or excellence (or both), in anything from sport to music, from debating to chess or bridge. And the opportunities for exercising those talents are there for the taking for hundreds who are young, enthusiastic and able. How good it is to see a student making use of such abilities; how sad to see one who gets the balance wrong, and gives too much time and energy to the recreational, or too much intensity to the academic side. Ah, yes: all work and no play makes Jack a dull boy and, presumably, *mutatis mutandis*, Jill an equally dull girl!

There is an odd company of people – of whom I am one – who find themselves at some period of life happily *in* a University ambience, but not actually *of* it. We constitute not, I trust, a lunatic fringe; no, more a collection of benign and interested moths, whose very last thought would be insolently to nibble at any academic gown! We revel in the light of others' learning, that's all; oh, where it is profound or incomprehensible we are dazzled, but where it is helpfully illuminating we rejoice. I have learned all sorts of details from students about many a subject, and was once even asked to read through an Engineering dissertation, though on the strict understanding that any observations be confined to the spelling, the syntax and the grammar! A certain reassurance has crept in, I admit, since I have come more and more to see that not everyone can do everything, and that no single campus luminary exemplifies the words of the famous musical:

> I can do anything better that you can,
> I can do anything better than you.

So those of us who do not now wholly belong to a University – though we *feel* we belong – should not be daunted or overwhelmed by the richness of the talents of those who do. There are inevitable, merciful limitations to everyone's gifts. Often the more gifted are the most reticent, and great minds seem normally to be free from pretentiousness. It is just possible, however, that a few in this Chapel may share a certain diffidence in the company of academic personages, or be a little tongue-tied in attempting to converse with them. In that case it does no harm to reflect that you may perhaps be able to perform quite ordinary tasks better than they can or at least as well as they can: you may be streets ahead of them when it comes to baking a cake, ironing, cleaning a car, or solving crossword puzzles! It *is* important for us not to undervalue the things we can do, nor to overvalue the things other people can do. The man in our Gospel passage who had one talent was not a problem because he had 'only' one talent, as opposed to the man with two or the one with five. Let's look at the passage afresh and see where the one-talent man was wrong.

We can start to understand our parable as soon as we

see that the essential requirement of the talents is working for God. You will have noticed that Our Lord keeps the same imagery of trading that he had used in the house of Zacchaeus at Jericho, though here he gives the idea a more spiritual tone. A talent was the largest unit of money in use; it represented several years' wages. So, large sums are in question here, as Jesus addresses his earliest disciples; but even these great riches are small compared to the reward paid for faithful service. There lies an obligation upon all who would follow him. People must *use* the sum entrusted to them, not let it lie idle; they must have God's interest at heart, not their own. This is especially clear in the case of the third servant, in other respects, presumably, a good man, for he did not spend his talent in riotous living; he did not waste it dishonestly; he was not in debt. He was not bad, merely negative. He did no wrong; he just did nothing at all. And that is why he is condemned. If we have that point settled, our otherwise sneaking inclination to sympathize with him should diminish. As Monsignor Ronald Knox once put it:

> The method of God's arithmetic is at odds with humankind's; for whereas with us $5+5=10$, and $2+2=4$, with God $1+0=0$.

I wonder if Jesus was directing the lesson of this third character at Judas, for the root of this man's trouble lay in his mistrusting not his own abilities, but the justice and generosity of his master. Judas shut his mind and heart to the goodness and love of Jesus; that is why he finally despaired. God evidently does not want men and women that are careful of their own personal security. They must, rather, be prepared to take risks. If they do not invest their spiritual credit, he gives it to others who will.

Yes, there are people who seem habitually to live in dispositions of servile fear of God. It's almost a state in which their offending him might hardly matter, but for their dread of his chastisement here or hereafter. It is their habit to regard God only as a master, a taskmaster, rather than to serve him, lovingly. Just like our one-talented friend in the parable. In a book called *Christ in His Mysteries*, first published some eighty years ago, Dom Columba Marmion wrote:

> Such souls act with God only at a distance; they treat with him only as with a great Lord, and God treats them in consequence according to this attitude. He does not give himself fully to them; between them and God, personal intimacy cannot exist; in them, inward expansion is impossible.

Dom Columba may have made his point a shade starkly, but it does look like being valid all the same.

Sometimes it's helpful to reflect upon this matter in another way: I mean, to consider people who have been deprived of some wonderful talent through accident or other misfortune: musicians, for example, their careers terminated while they were at the height of their powers – like the cellist Jacqueline du Pré, or the pianist Solomon. A great poet of the sixteenth century, John Milton, was afflicted with blindness as a comparatively young man, and composed a sonnet reflecting on the circumstance. Referring in it directly to our parable of this morning, he speaks of

> ... *that one talent* which is death to hide,
> Lodged with me useless, though my soul more bent

To serve therewith my Maker, and present
My true account, lest he, returning, chide.

But then he goes on to consider the virtue of patience in the face of tribulation, and ends with the famous line:

They also serve, who only stand and wait.

(Wait upon, that is, not wait for.) Service, then, that is the key word, service rooted in patience and dedication; a willingness to work on and on, even when, as in the case of Milton, the greatest gift there once was has been removed. Anyone who has listened to the Radio 4 programme *In Touch* will know how tremendous is the resourcefulness of blind people in general when it comes to facing up to and making the most of life – with courage and, nearly always, humour. Indeed handicapped folk as a whole leave the rest of us often a long way behind in the full usage of the residual talents they do have, or else have developed, in spite of or even as a result of their disability.

Quite often students discover during their University years gifts or aptitudes they never thought they had. Maybe a friend introduces them to a sport or pastime they find they enjoy. Or maybe something in their curriculum stimulates their zeal through a book read or a lecture given – perhaps even in an 'optional' course initially undertaken to fill in the timetable. I have certainly known students who came into Theology with a school record of some mediocrity, but who took to some part of their studies, at least, like proverbial ducks to water. Imagine the benefit this could have later in their ministerial work, for themselves and for those they

would serve ... But let me give you a slightly different
instance. This particular lad had been a quite ordinary
student at Blairs College, the then Junior Seminary, near
Aberdeen, and had gone straight on to the Scots College
in Rome to pursue his studies for the priesthood. He
decided to take a side-course in Latin at the Gregorian
University, where the lecturer was a bright American
scholar, whose normal work was preparing and editing
the Latin originals of important Vatican documents. His
teaching abilities were marvellous, and his knack of
inspiring enthusiasm in his pupils quite uncanny. At any
rate, our young student immersed himself in Fr Foster's
material, almost to the point of obsession, and became
highly expert in this area. He decided after a few years
not to continue at the College; came home, sat the
Glasgow Entrance Bursary, gained a good placing, and
proceeded to take an Honours degree in Latin and Greek
with the greatest of ease! All to the great advantage of
his present pupils, and thanks to a kind of academic
afterthought that enabled his classical talents to emerge.

Clearly, the Christian way is to make use of our
talents to the greater honour and glory of God, and
hence to employ them not towards our own vain glory,
but to let them work for us in godly service for the
benefit of our neighbour. You must have come across
plenty of people like that in your own experience – at
school, perhaps, or here in St Andrews. One who
springs to mind is a former chaplain at Aberdeen
University, with whom I was at school (around the dawn
of history!). He, and indeed his brother David, had all
the gifts you could imagine – at sport and in study, and
became captains of this and that all the way through.
Now my friend would hate my eulogizing him, of

course, but I mention him as someone who gave
everything he had, everything he believed in for the
good of the community – coming eventually to the
ministry in which for some years his talents were
abundantly available. With words he was particularly
masterly, as anyone who heard his sermons or prayers,
or read even his simplest writings, would attest.

And so we come back to this estimable and ancient
University, with two things much in mind. Firstly, how
over all the centuries this foundation has been a
storehouse of wisdom, and through the industry of its
alumni has distributed countless talents at home and
overseas; and secondly, how in this pre-millennial year
the task has fallen anew upon us to do likewise, most of
all upon you who are yet young and in your full vigour.
There is a powerful hymn, used from time to time on
days of graduation, whose first verse begins:

> Lord, in the fullness of my might
> I would for thee be strong.

and whose final verse succinctly presents an offering of
youthful talents:

> O choose me in my golden time;
> In my dear joys have part!
> For thee the glory of my prime,
> The fullness of my heart.

If the spirit of those lines is a part of our living, we
cannot behave like our man in the parable who buried his
one talent. Rather, we shall stand at the last before Our
Lord with the wishful confidence contained in the family

motto of Aberdeen University's pious founder, Bishop Elphinstone: *non confundar* – 'may I not be put to shame' – and shall hope to hear the Master say, even to you and me:

'Well done, good and faithful servant.'

Note
1.   Preached in St Salvator's Chapel, University of St Andrews.

Southwark Sermon

The sacrifice of God is a troubled spirit. A broken and contrite heart, O God, thou shalt not despise. (*Psalm 51*)

Fifty years ago, at school in Edinburgh, my class started to read Chaucer. One of the early lines in the Prologue runs: 'In Southwark at the Tabard as I lay'. I haven't given Southwark much thought in the meantime, but much of the Prologue has stayed in my mind – about that band of pilgrims setting out from here to Canterbury six hundred years ago, and telling their tales. Oh, the Friar, the Pardoner and others show little evidence of broken and contrite hearts; yet in many of the pilgrims there are points of character, now haughty, now humble, where we probably recognize ourselves! Only the poor Parson and his brother the Ploughman escape the author's satire.

It was a real ploughman of a later time, Robert Burns, who visited *his* ridicule upon those he thought were hypocrites, especially in matters of religion. Here, for instance, is the dissembling Holy Willie addressing his Maker:

> I bless and praise thy matchless might
> When thousands thou hast left in night
> That I am here afore thy sight
> For gifts an' grace
> A burnin' an' a shinin' light
> To a' this place.

And the poem's title? 'Holy Willie's *Prayer*'! And we think, how droll! Yet it's perfectly possible for us to delude ourselves even when we pray. Father Jock Dalrymple, that exemplary Scottish priest, came to suspect, after many years' ministry, that he'd been more in love with prayer than with God. Probably we too have preferred at times to take centre-stage and consign the Almighty to the wings.

The battle goes on, in all of us, between pride and humility; and the lines can be blurred at times, the vice seeming almost to be the virtue. The devil knows what he is about. Screwtape and his henchmen dislike un-employment! Remember that line in Genesis: 'now the serpent was more subtle than any beast of the field.' So when we protest we're of no account, or that we're misery itself and nothing but refuse, how would we like to be taken at our word, and have this said of us by others?

A waggish friend, an Anglican, remarked to me recently: 'Yes, I do so admire humility – in other people!' And so perhaps do you and I! After all, to have *our* hearts bruised or crushed could involve a degree of discomfort – even pain – which we'd rather do without! A troubled spirit, a humble, contrite heart: how elusive it is for the honest seeker, how hard to discern. Hilaire Belloc's epigram fairly hits the mark:

> I said to Heart: how goes it?
> Heart replied: Right as a Ribstone Pippin; but it lied.

I remember an eminent cardiologist opening a talk with this word from Jeremiah: 'The heart is deceitful above all things, who can know it?' This is surely as true of the spiritual as of the physical side.

The author of Psalm 51 – possibly King David repenting

of his adultery with Bathsheba – has a series of telling insights into the affairs of the heart. And he comes before God with a number of stark imperatives: have mercy, blot out, wash me, purge me, and so on. There's urgency as well as realism about his highly personal prayer, self-abasement included. Yes, just occasionally it's proper almost to grovel as he does when we pray, to come before the Almighty, slime of the earth that each of us is, and admit 'Lord, my name is mud!' His conviction of the need for drastic measures led John Donne to cry out:

Batter my heart, three-personed God, for you
As yet but knock, breathe, shine, and seek to mend;
That I may rise and stand, o'erthrow me, and bend
Your force to break, blow, burn and make me whole.

Indeed our sin is ever before us; so is our waywardness, our dallying with temptation. The battering-ram of God's insistent love *alone* will crush our underlying pride.

For all that, humility shouldn't make permanent doormats of us, mud or no mud! It shouldn't oblige us to think less of ourselves than of others, or have a low opinion of our gifts. Perfect humility would mean freedom from thinking about ourselves one way or the other at all! Disinterest in self would lead us to focus our thinking and our acting on the needs of other people, for humility is charity's first cousin. St Francis de Sales, for all his *douceur*, teases us about our self-importance even at surface level: 'Some people are proud,' he declares, 'because they ride a fine horse, or have a feather in their hat, or are very well dressed. This is obvious folly, for if there is any glory here it belongs to the horse or the bird or the tailor!'

Psalm 51 is an exercise in self-examination, transparently candid. The desire to be cleansed is intense, for the consciousness of sin oppresses its author. 'Wash me thoroughly,' he begs, 'create in me a clean heart.' And the whole poem, in its prayerful power, challenges us in *our* struggle to be open, to be lowly in God's sight. And it sets before us, with a rising degree of optimism, ideals that would be within our grasp, if only we'd put ourselves meekly in God's hands, if only we'd trust his loving-kindness. Neither burnt-offering nor any other external show of service will suffice. Only a troubled spirit, only a change of heart will do. And with delicious diffidence the psalmist is hopeful that God will *not despise* his bruised, repentant being. A lovely touch of courtesy, this, arising from his penitence.

Mind you, we can spend so much time in trying to eliminate the great *I am* that we may become vainly anxious, even scrupulous about it. Humour is a helpful corrective. So I like to remember the seventeenth-century Scottish peer, Lord Erskine, who complained to his publisher about the tardy production of his auto-biography. He was told that the printers had sadly run out of capital 'I's!

If we've found our text, our psalm useful, if its message and beauty have moved us, we should make it our own, commit it to memory. Even C. S. Lewis tells us of *his* habit of 'festooning' his prayers with personal thoughts that bring out the force of originals *for him*. Scholarship, tradition, received piety, all have their place. But for you, for me, in our quest for forgiveness, only your heart, only mine can *individually* respond. And, in so far as they *do* respond, we shall gradually inch our way forward to holiness.

Mercifully and from time to time there *are* saints among and around us: good, godly people in every walk of life. Their humility shines when it catches the light: the one who's affronted and feels it's no more than is deserved; the one who assumes the successful rival was the better choice for a promoted post; or who'll work with a will to the plans of others when they run contrary to his or her advice – and a hundred other instances. Saints present and past – of Old and New Testament times – illumine in great matters and in small the penitential twilight. Among them is your London-born Thomas à Becket, whose shrine Chaucer's pilgrims, and *real* pilgrims too, went to Canterbury 'the holy, blisful martyr for to seke'. Consonant with our theme, pointing up our text, are these words from T. S. Eliot's play about him: 'The true martyr is he who has become the instrument of God, who has lost his will in the will of God, and who no longer desires anything for himself, not even the glory of being a martyr.'

A Scattering of Published Sermonettes

Tell me where is fancy bred,
Or in the heart, or in the head?
How begot, how nourished?
Reply, reply.
(Shakespeare, *The Merchant of Venice*, III, 2, 63ff)

From time to time over the past few years the Aberdeen *Press and Journal* has asked me to contribute to its 'Saturday Sermon' column. Pieces are limited to five hundred words, and the writer is free to choose any topic thought to be helpful or stimulating to the reader.

Imagining, let alone knowing, who or of what kind the latter may be is hard. However, the challenge is to attempt to compose a piece with spiritual content without denominational slant yet Christian in essence.

The use of literary allusions has come readily to me in this task, and my efforts have fallen into what Nicholas Boyle would call 'nonpurposive', written purely to please. On looking over the seventy sermonettes originally offered, I am at least content to have expressed not only thoughts that enthuse me, but thoughts too intended to be of pastoral support to others.

The first two given here are based upon my zeal for drama since boyhood. It is suggesting briefly how 'all the world's a stage', and ends with lines designed to offer encouragement.

Another sermon tries to show how Voice and Verse can and do offer delight and variety to the lives of many, what I call 'solace to the human spirit and a means towards its deepest welfare'.

Yet another piece deals as diplomatically as possible with the problem of sloth, and incorporates not only secular authors and their reflections, but also some lines from the book of Proverbs. It is hoped that such a synthesis of the secular and the sacred will achieve its end!

Others were influenced by thoughts on topics as diverse as the season of the year; the need to catch the beauty of the passing moment; the human desire for peace and restfulness; the human pride (often misplaced!) in academic accomplishment; the onset of age; and, of especial moment to a preacher, the problem of inopportune sore throats!

Drama

Many of us in our youth became happily involved in drama. This may have stood us in good stead in later life by enabling us to conquer 'nerves' when obliged to speak in public.

It would do this by teaching us how to project the voice in spacious surroundings or, most important of all, by giving us the stimulus to work as a team in unity of zeal and purpose.

In a large cast (often the norm in a school or college), togetherness wasn't merely laudable; it was central to the whole operation. Some of the actors were much better than others, but there was no question of rooting out the 'weakest link', for everyone knew that the smallest of roles, even that of the so-called extras, was crucial in the quest to achieve as high a standard as possible. Petty jealousies were entirely verboten.

I have a favourite recollection of a boy who revelled in minor parts and was regarded as mildly eccentric. He even assumed a stage name, George Hindmarsh.

A few years later, he astounded us by gaining the Military Cross in the Korean War. Had his stage experiences anything to do with building up his confidence?

I think, too, of the drunken porter in Macbeth who was to become a luminary in the medical world, or of the boy who played Bluebeard in Saint Joan and rose in due time to become a British ambassador.

It would be folly to read too much into this. Yet, in the first case dealing with people and in the second dealing diplomatically with governments might have been eased fractionally as a result of those embryonic communication skills.

Our unconventional producer in those far-off days was the late Scott Allan. His special ability lay not only in his deep understanding of the plays themselves (usually Shakespeare or Shaw), but in imparting his zest to boys who were willing enough to learn, and who in the end could amaze themselves and others by giving performances of youthful but real distinction. Teamwork and self-expression: how gloriously complementary they are and how vital for adult maturity. Add to that the need for discipline and loyalty within a young cast and we have two qualities by no means conspicuous among grown-ups of our time and place.

To look upon life as a drama is no new insight, but to try to discern our proper and personal role within it is hard. Many of us made our first entrance long ago. We have fluffed or forgotten our lines times without number, and often spoken from a script of which we were ashamed.

Yet a talent for acting is a gift from God, whose love will not fail us up to and beyond the final curtain. He is the ultimate author.

Consider for comfort these lines of Francis Quarles:

> My soul, sit thou a patient looker-on;
> Judge not the play before the play is done:
> Her plot has many changes; every day
> Speaks a new scene; the last act crowns the play.

Characters

In a sense we're all actors. Though we may not follow Shakespeare's 'seven ages' as described by the melancholy Jaques, we do all share in life's drama, that maddeningly unpredictable mixture of tragedy and comedy. Hilaire Belloc took a cynical tone in affirming:

> The scenery is very much the best
> Of what the wretched drama has to show,
> Also the prompter happens to be dumb;
> Then, before we go,
> Loud cries for 'Author', but he doesn't come.

Mind you, the scenery is important. Many of the saints would bear this out, not least Francis of Assisi, plus a multitude of writers (poets especially), who've seen in the beauty of the natural world a reflection of the beauty of God himself. Gerard Manley Hopkins, thrilled by the contrasts within the loveliness of creation, saw it as a secondary cause for worship: 'He fathers forth whose beauty is past change. Praise him!'

There are passages in Scripture which are of the very stuff of drama, like certain Old Testament narratives (David and Goliath, Abraham and Isaac, and many others). The New Testament too portrays much in dramatic style (the raising of Lazarus or the taking of the woman in adultery, for example). Our Lord himself presents some of his parables almost in theatrical vein. The sheep and the goats or the unjust steward spring to mind.

If parts of the public ministry of Christ often come across like scenes within a lengthy play, this is supremely true of the Passion, where episode builds upon episode in a relentless drama acted out, as it were, against a backcloth of royal purple.

There's an uncomfortable parallel at times between the actions of some minor characters and our own. Content to feel at one with Simon of Cyrene, the centurion or the good thief, we nonetheless feel an unnerving affinity with Peter in his denials, Pilate in his pusillanimity, or even Judas in his betrayal.

Romano Guardini boldly arraigns us regarding the latter: 'We have little cause to speak of "the traitor" with indignation as someone far away and long ago,' he writes. 'Judas unmasks us.' And a mask is an actor's disguise. We should ask God not to let the treacheries of which we've been guilty become rooted within us.

Some may be understandably uplifted by this sidelight on our sorry scene expressed by G. K. Chesterton:

> Men say the sun was darkened, yet I had
> Thought it beat brightly, even on – Calvary:
> And he that hung upon the torturing tree
> Heard all the crickets sing, and was glad.

Another poet, Francis Quarles, brings us back gently and reflectively to our theme of drama:

> My soul, sit thou a patient looker-on
> Judge not the play, before the play is done:
> Her plot has many changes; every day
> Speaks a new scene; the last act crowns the play.

A judgement on the play you and I have acted in would meantime be inappropriate. Judgement on the performers must be left to God.

Voice and Verse

Let's start with lines by John Milton:

> Blest pair of Sirens, pledges of Heaven's joy,
> Sphere-born harmonious
> Sisters, Voice and Verse.

The Sirens of Greek mythology lived on a rocky island to which they would lure seafarers with their lovely singing. However, we'll look on them as symbols representing the sheer beauty of music and poetry. May they still provide enchantment for their devotees, but without peril or entrapment.

Most of us will have known the attraction of a fine piece of music here, a memorable poem there. Often, the delight will have started in our schooldays, thanks to an inspiring teacher or fellow-pupil whose zeal was infectious.

Again, someone within the family circle has had a gift for spoken or instrumental expression and those efforts, heard or overheard, may have set us on the road to wider discoveries.

We might never be active musicians or reciters ourselves, but all may have the joy of listening to words and music rendered giftedly by others. This is especially true these days, with so many technical aids and contraptions to hand. Yet there's really no substitute for a 'live' performance.

Spiritual uplift may come to us in any guise, from a song to a symphony, from a poem to a play, whether the piece is overtly religious or not. Indeed, there is a wealth of inspiration to be had from the great tradition of Anglican choral music or the polyphony of Palestrina, from incomparable sections of the Bible or the poems of George Herbert, but our emotions can be engaged and our hearts moved by the works of those whose aim was solely artistic.

Occasionally, a professedly agnostic composer may respond brilliantly to the challenge of producing, say, important hymn-tunes: Vaughan Williams, for instance.

Recently, the BBC radio programme *Desert Island Discs* celebrated its sixtieth birthday. A good number of specifically religious pieces had cropped up over the years, but the elusive 'tingle factor' had swayed many of the illustrious castaways in their choice of records.

And who are we to want to restrict the effects of the Holy Spirit to only the holier types of Sirenic utterance? The Devil might *want* to have all the best tunes (and the most persuasive poetry), but the energy and fire of the finest music and verse cannot but bring serenity and strength to a person's soul.

Anything, then, from Gregorian plainchant to a Beethoven concerto on the one hand, or from a holy sonnet of Donne to a powerful scene from Shakespeare on the other, can be a solace to the human spirit and a means towards its deepest welfare.

Some people have admitted that the glory of certain passages has been actually painful in its impact, almost too much to bear. Personally, I find that the slow movements of perfect symphonies affect me so, and most of the poems of Gerard Manley Hopkins.

Thanks be to God for the richly varied genius of the great musicians and poets of every age.

Sloth

Finding time to read for pleasure is often difficult. However, I succeeded during the Christmas period in tackling one of the unread book-tokened presents of months ago. It was the *Oxford Book of Essays*.

Now, essays are things one read ages ago at school, things at times endured rather than enjoyed. Mind you, some of Charles Lamb's pieces were quite fun. Do you remember *The Superannuated Man*, for example, or the *Dissertation upon Roast Pig*?

Well, there's a fine essay in my book by a contemporary of Lamb called Leigh Hunt. He was, in his day, a prolific writer, mainly of poetry and drama. He also supported a number of friends who were later to become far more famous than himself, including Keats and Byron.

Hunt's whimsical sense of humour comes out well in his essay, which I've thoroughly relished, entitled *Getting up on Cold Mornings*. He puts with urbanity the case for and against the practice of staying in bed on winter mornings.

Having asked the reader how this conduct can be indulged in by a rational being, he declares 'How? Why, with the argument calmly at work in one's head and the clothes over one's shoulder.'

In another vein, he points out that the poets, 'refining upon the tortures of the damned, make one of their greatest agonies consist in being suddenly transported from heat to cold, from fire to ice.' Surely this is a reference to Dante, among others.

Nevertheless, Hunt does admit to a weakness in this

presentation. The lier-in might actually make life terribly awkward for other people, by upsetting their plans for breakfast, for instance, or making the tidying up of the house nearly impossible.

There's the rub, for how can the lazybones reconcile his selfish inaction with the precept about loving one's neighbour?

The Book of Proverbs is uncompromising in dealing with feeble excuses for unacceptable behaviour.

In our present regard, take these two texts: 'Yet a little sleep, a little slumber, a little folding of the hands to sleep: so shall thy poverty come as one that travelleth, and thy want as an armed man.'

And again: 'As the door turneth upon its hinges, so doth the slothful upon his bed.' You can almost sense the creaking not only of the door, but of the anatomical joints as well.

It's clear that our essayist's lightsome touch has to be adjusted in respect of deeper, spiritual lessons. If private sloth amid the warm bedclothes is to be challenged, let it be in the name of charity towards others.

There is still a gentlemanly custom in monasteries by which the monk on duty arouses his brethren with bell-ringing and the early cry *Benedicamus Domino* ('Let us bless the Lord'); to which gracious greeting the reply from within the cell is *Deo gratias* ('Thanks be to God').

I wonder how many of us would be able to attain, on a chilly morn, half that level of courtesy, or even a quarter, and even at New Year?

November Evenings

Another October all but over, another November to be faced. Longer nights, shorter days and time for reflection.

We bid farewell to autumn, ruminating nostalgically upon the 'season of mists and mellow fruitfulness' immortalized by Keats. He died young, and his own sad epitaph declares: 'Here lies one whose name was writ in water.' Happily Keats was mistaken, for his life and his lines have been championed and interpreted ever since by an array of admiring poetry-lovers.

One of the first to support him was his contemporary Shelley, that complex and wayward genius. Take these lines from his elegy upon Keats, *Adonais*:

> He is made one with Nature: there is heard
> His voice in all her music, from the moan
> Of thunder, to the song of the night's sweet bird.

Many who enjoy reading may spend their November evenings immersed in a novel or biography or history, attuning their mood to the darker notes of 'night's sweet bird' (the nightingale, surely).

Others, however, may find their solace through the verses and insights of great poetry, where the keen searcher is free to pore over a lengthier work or to alight upon something more concise. No Shakespeare or Milton, no R. S. Thomas or Emily Dickinson – it is all a matter of temperament and whim.

Most of us who are elderly were brought up on poems to be learned by heart, some of which we may have loathed, while others will have taken root deep within us, to be recalled and appreciated repeatedly over the years.

Two of my favourite anthologies are Walter de la Mare's *Come Hither*, so Keatsian in its celebration of nature, and Francis Meynell's *By Heart*. On the flyleaf of the latter I inscribed, many years ago, these words: 'This book was meant to be a present for ... but she was too ill for presents. May she rest in peace.'

Each compiler was conscious of the bond between poetry and youth. Indeed de la Mare subtitles his volume, 'For the young of all ages', while Meynell quotes Robert Frost's dictum that no poetry is good for the young that is not equally good for their elders.

On the matter of memory, Meynell adds that the no-longer-young often read poems they thought they had forgotten, only to find that they can retrieve them almost word for word.

During the bombings of World War II, Beatrice Ward wrote a poem graphically endorsing the value of learning poetry by heart. Part of it ran:

> Soon you must play your part.
> What are you learning?
> Get it by heart. By heart!
> I have seen books burning.

Meynell then pleads, in words as applicable to our times as to his: 'May the need for that warning never recur. May peace be in the world, and poetry in your heart.'

Amen to that, not least because, like all lovely things, the beauty of poetry redounds to the glory of God, whose beauty is absolute.

Spelling

Poet George Herbert made these cautionary remarks about sermons:

> God calleth preaching folly. Do not grudge
> To pick out treasures from an earthen pot.
> The worst speaks something good;
> If all want sense,
> God takes a text and preacheth patience.

Clergy, please note.

Given that preaching's essence is the proclamation of the word of God, it has certain accompaniments that can be helpful: presentation skills, for instance, or correct pronunciation, or careful grammar.

However, one factor in a sermon's preparation which a congregation cannot know is whether or not the preacher is a competent speller.

One may be adept, another not. I nearly said 'skilful', a favourite word of mine ever since I spelled it right, sixty-five years ago in an oral exam at a primary school where my mother was keen I should enter.

Senior citizens, as a rule, will have been trained to spell correctly through repeated testing, with dire consequences for failure. Later generations, especially those of the 1960s and 1970s, may have escaped such demanding standards, with the result that even luminaries of the law and of medicine have been less than proficient spellers. Nor are the clergy immune.

Yet even if we think we can spell correctly, we should avoid self-praise. There are bound to be weaknesses in our armoury. Unaccountably, certain words will send us fleeing to a dictionary to make quite sure how a word should go. I have a nervousness about the words 'achievement', 'acknowledgement', and 'nucleus'. I have just checked them again. You might have word-traps, too.

Enthusiasts have tried in the past to simplify English spelling, Bernard Shaw and Dr Mont Follick among them. Indeed, for people struggling with our language as foreigners, we should have every sympathy. Take a word like 'rough'. Set alongside it 'bough', 'cough' and 'dough'. Then try reconciling the spelling and the pronunciation. It's impossible.

Still, there's a danger of pedantry, of being over-fussy in this whole area. Remember Sam Weller's response to the judge in Pickwick Papers on being asked to provide his surname:

'Do you spell it with a V or a W?'
'That depends upon the taste and fancy of the speller, my
    Lord.'

Mind you, shouldn't we feel a touch of shame in resorting regularly to spell-checks, or quail a little when our noble tongue is demeaned by the codified gibberish of text-messages?

Returning to our friend George Herbert, we find in his poem *The Flower*, in which he reflects upon the vicissitudes of his own life, these lines addressing God:

We say amiss
This or that is:
Thy word is all, if we could spell.

The writer might have had in mind the Scriptures as a whole, or in particular the coming among us of the Word made flesh. Worthily to adore the latter is, for a Christian, something to be essayed and longed for, and so, with Charles Wesley, we exclaim:

> O for a thousand tongues, to sing
> My great Redeemer's praise,
> The glories of my God and King,
> The triumphs of his grace.

A Sore Throat

I am exhausted with calling out: my throat is hoarse.
(Psalm 69)

A woman in Jane Austen's *Persuasion* declares: 'My sore throats are always worse than anyone's.' Indeed, those whose anatomical weak spot is the pharynx or larynx might readily homologate that view.

Although a sore throat carries little glamour and is unlikely to enlist sought-after sympathy, to the patient it has much more than nuisance value, especially when it affects the vocal cords.

Hoarseness is not only embarrassing, it might acutely involve problems of communication, not least in churches. In pre-microphone days, there was a condition commonly called 'clergyman's throat'.

Such maladies so constrict the use of the voice that singing and shouting become sorely difficult. Thence flows the matter of considerateness for others, who might sigh gratefully that we've been debarred meantime from melodic activity and from the possibility of raising our voices, either through mirth or rage.

Remedies, real or alleged, abound, from the old-fashioned but effective gargling with salted water to the use of the latest lozenges or liquids, including varieties of 'linctus', a syrupy mixture derivatively requiring to be licked up. Ugh. Personally, I'd recommend a warm milk with honey in it.

Enforced silence can be indirectly beneficial at times, since it might bring with it a necessary withdrawal from the daily hurly-burly, and a consequent tranquillity of spirit. It may afford us the chance to reflect peacefully and purposefully about the things in our lives that really matter.

Call it a quiet time if you will, or even a private retreat. Where prayer is concerned, sore-throatedness may give us a great opportunity for thoughtful, personal meditation, although excellent Christians could doubtless ponder the eternal truths, regardless of the state of their throats.

At any rate, underlying silence there's a spiritual quality leading us into God's presence intimately, perhaps intensely. Take John G. Whittier's lovely words:

> With that deep hush subduing all
> Our words and works that drown
> The tender whisper of thy call,
> As noiseless let thy blessing fall
> As fell thy manna down.

Setting aside a daily time for quiet prayer is a habit tried and proven in many a holy life. Faithfulness and regularity in its practice are of the essence. Not that we should ever jettison spoken prayer, either in private or public, although much may be said for the dictum of Thomas Carlyle: 'Under all speech that is good for anything, there lies a silence that is better.'

Didn't the great Elijah experience God's presence not in wind, earthquake or fire, but in 'a still, small voice'?

Incidentally, care of the throat has been vested by Christian piety in a saint called Blaise, an early Armenian bishop. More power to his spatula. The name appears in St Blazey in Cornwall and in parts of Germany.

Pharyngeal problems might be rampant there but, given our local climate, his patronage would not go amiss here, either, 'amid the uncertain glory of an April day' (Shakespeare).

Each Day

The poet James Russell Lowell once penned these lovely seasonal words:

> And what is so rare as a day in June?
> Then, if ever, come perfect days,
> Then Heaven tries earth if it be in tune,
> And over it softly her warm ear lays.

Our hope is strong that this June month will be a fine one. Sports people, not to mention prospective holidaymakers, will be studying the weather forecasts with particular care.

Yet it would be a mistake to look too far ahead, for there's much to be said for approaching every single day as if it were special, be it in June or not.

The serene St Francis of Assisi advised his followers to greet each new dawn as if it were a birthday present from God. Is that view a touch unrealistic? It might seem to be so in our workaday world, with its unremitting stress and its focus upon material things.

And there's the rub, for it might be that we've grown so used to our busyness that we've crowded out any available time for quiet reflection. So even a glorious June day can run its course with scant admiration on our part.

Do we really need to be at sport or on holiday to stop and give a moment or two to godly thoughts of praise and thanksgiving? An awareness of God's created gifts is proclaimed most famously by Jesus in the Sermon on the Mount, but there's an extra insight in the Letter to the

Hebrews, in which it states: 'Every day, so long as this today lasts, keep encouraging one another.'

Our Christian duty, therefore, goes far beyond prayers for our own intentions, for we must want to share with others our gladness in the blessings of each day. More than that, the word 'encouraging' in our quotation suggests that our concern should be especially for people whose day or days are clouded by bereavement, doubt, pain, poverty and a hundred other hardships. After all, it's love of God and love of neighbour that beckon us along the road to perfection.

Perfection – a splendid ideal, but the misuse of our free will keeps leading us into sin. Yet instead of fretting about whether or not we shall ever commit sins again, why don't we resolve, with God's help, not to commit them today?

Throughout today, let us strive to keep the freshness and innocence of a beauteous morning in our hearts. In the words of the mystic St Gertrude: 'We should offer our heart to God every day as a rose with the dew still on it.'

It may be helpful to be specific, according to the vagaries of our temperament. For example, if we're likely to be waylaid by folk we find tiresome, today, for a change, we'll greet them as brothers and sisters, with unfeigned and infectious cheerfulness, thus lightening their burden as well as our own. A kindly smile – even that might make a difference for someone who is sad or sorrowful this June morning.

Greenness

> Fair daffodils, we weep to see
> You haste away so soon.

So wrote the poet Robert Herrick. The citizens of Aberdeen can echo that sentiment each year about this time, as the glorious invasion of thousands of these flowers becomes a sad retreat.

People will have their favourite areas of display – South Anderson Drive, maybe, or the grassy terraces around the hospital at Foresterhill.

Indeed, the pity about most flowers is that they last so short a time and look so sorrowful in their reluctant demise. Similarly, in a church context, the floral decorations and bouquets at weddings, or the tributes at funerals, are destined soon to wither.

Yet, in a lovely manner, the flowers are important symbols, of hope in the case of matrimony, of love where death has come. With regard to the latter, the poet George Herbert wrote a charming piece called *The Flower* in which he described the human soul's recovering greenness in the sense that a flower goes under the earth in winter to return from its roots in the spring – an image of the soul's revival, and survival, after death.

Many of us may identify with his question:

> Who would have thought my shrivelled heart
> Could have recovered greenness?
> It was gone quite underground.

The poet yearns thereafter to be safe in paradise, where no flower can decay. Still, he is conscious of his continual unworthiness, but, in the end, hope and trust bring recompense, even in this life.

For Herbert, this has meant a return to his craft of verse-writing, his best delight:

> And now in age I bud again,
> After so many deaths I live and write;
> I once more smell the dew and rain,
> And relish versing.

All very well, we may say, where there's a glad outcome. However, many a time for many a one, hope seems scant and reassurance difficult to grasp. Remember the cry of another poet-genius, the depressive Gerard Manley Hopkins, amid his personal slough of despond:

> Why do sinners' ways prosper? And why must
> Disappointment all I endeavour end?

Spring in this country coincides with Eastertide, so we move from the serious weeks of Lent into a spiritual springtime, culminating in the festival of Christ's resurrection. Therein lies the very core of our believing.

St Paul put it thus in his first letter to the Corinthians, chapter 15: 'If there be no resurrection of the dead, then is Christ not risen: And if Christ be not risen, then is our preaching vain, and your faith is also vain ... But now is Christ risen from the dead, and become the first-fruits of them that slept' (KJB).

Therefore we should rejoice, with the ancient cry of

Alleluia on our lips and in our hearts, for (in the fine imagery of a contemporary hymn):

> Now the green blade riseth from the buried grain,
> Wheat that in the dark earth many days has lain.

Far better than a host of golden daffodils. *Surrexit Dominus de sepulcro*. 'The Lord has arisen from the tomb!'

Aging

John Earle was an Anglican bishop in the seventeenth century. A worthy churchman, his reputation now depends less on his ministry than upon a collection of character sketches he wrote entitled *Microcosmographie*. It's indebted to pieces by the ancient Greek philosopher and botanist Theophrastus. The tone is gentle and whimsical, in a work composed (some say) as a counterbalance to the harsher cameos of his choleric contemporary Sir Thomas Overbury.

Earle's essay *A Good Old Man* is a masterly portrait in miniature, as generous as it is observant. Its language recalls that of the Authorized Version of the Bible and, in particular, the book of Proverbs, so full of wisdom and balance. Indeed, to someone like the present writer, past the allotted span of three-score years and ten, Earle offers some comfort, as well as room for self-assessment.

There's a moment in Shakespeare's *As You Like It* when the young hero addresses the serving-man, Adam, thus: 'O good old man, how well in thee appears/The constant service of the antique world.' (Act II, Scene III)

Earle praises his aged subject similarly: 'One whom time hath been thus long-a-working, and like winter fruit ripened when others are shaken down.'

The fact of belonging to the elderly is apt to be ignored, if not denied. It's understandable (we maintain) how other folk strain under the weight of years, but you or I cannot possibly be as bald, stout or decrepit as these individuals we grew up with, our fellow-students at school or college. We eschew obituary notices and consider the mirror a trickster. However, if we challenge ourselves less on the physical, more on the behavioural side, we find subterfuge harder. Earle commends his gentlemen who 'can distinguish gravity from a sour look, and the less testy he is, the more regarded'. Substitute for 'testy' the good old Scots word 'carnaptious' and see whether or not we can identify.

There's a popular saying, 'age doesn't come alone', since various infirmities of body and spirit accompany time's passage. Still, there are compensations, above all when the 'generation gap', far from being a problem, is something graciously affirming. Earle says of his subject: 'He practises his experience on youth without the harshness of reproof, and in his counsel is good company.' There is, indeed, a palpable beauty in a loving relationship of grandparents and grandchildren; and parents must often rejoice in the unstressed and supportive role of aunts and uncles, too.

The author of Ecclesiastes, scarcely a treatise on cheerfulness, qualifies even his brighter statements:

> However many years you live, enjoy them all; but remember, the days of darkness will be many: futility awaits you at the end (11:8).

Optimistically, we may accord better with Robert Browning's invitation in 'Rabbi Ben Ezra':

> Grow old along with me!
> The best is yet to be,
> The last of life,
> for which the first was made.

May we all press on heavenwards in hope, and may God take us home at the last.

The Passing Moment

Can you remember the first poem you enjoyed, or the one you were first compelled to learn at school?

For many of my generation, a little piece written by someone born on yesterday's date (April 25) in 1873 would be a likely candidate: *Silver*, by Walter de la Mare. I can still hear my mother's beautifully attuned voice reciting it, maybe in an effort to encourage me to do likewise.

> Slowly, silently, now the moon
> Walks the night in her silver shoon.

The imagery moves on with fluent simplicity till we reach the lovely ending.

> And moveless fish in the water gleam
> By silver reeds in a silver stream.

On my list of favourite bards there's another name to be mentioned, and that's the Welsh poet and clergyman of our era, R. S. Thomas. Mind you, you have to approach his work on a day when life seems relatively pleasant, for he often gives us thoughts that are sad, foreboding, or quite pessimistic.

Even his spiritual convictions appear to wobble from time to time. Yet the darker side can be offset by the brighter. For example, in a brief lyric called *The Bright Field*, based on verses in St Matthew's Gospel (13:45-6):

> Again, the kingdom of heaven is like unto a merchant man, seeking goodly pearls who, when he had found one pearl of great price, went and sold all that he had, and bought it.

Thomas opens quite simply.

> I have seen the sun break through
> to illuminate a small field for a while, and gone
>   my way
> and forgotten it.

He then goes on to stress the need not to forget such moments, but rather to treasure them as something precious that will not come again.

Moses, the poet avers, had just such a vision when faced with the burning bush. He turned aside to 'a brightness that seems as transitory as your youth once, but is the eternity that awaits you'.

Many a versifier, from the time of Horace and before, has praised the impulse to seize the beauty of the passing moment. Horace was essentially a poet and only a dabbler in politics.

Andrew Marvell, a seventeenth-century English poet who championed the same theme, became a professional politician in later life, but not before composing some masterly lyrics, including *To His Coy Mistress* (whose identity, and even existence, is doubtful):

> But at my back I always hear
> Time's winged chariot hurrying near;
> And yonder all before us lie
> Deserts of vast eternity.

Walter de la Mare's childlike genius grasped all that, and illustrated it repeatedly for our delight. Thanks be to God.

Carrying the Cross

We'll be entering the season of Lent shortly, the time of preparation for Easter. Among our tasks will be these: to attempt to follow Christ in that self-denial and self-giving which led him to Calvary, and to try, with his help, to get the better of our pride and selfishness, which are wholly at variance with his teaching and example.

Lent will clearly be a struggle, a wrestling between good and evil, but it should be stimulating. After all, the Lord, who bore his cross, has told us that, if we would come along his way, we, too, must carry the cross individually. If we share his suffering, we shall also share his glory. The fight is on.

To discover what our cross is will be harder for some than for others. People in chronic sickness or pain, those recently bereaved, the poor or marginalized – such are the fold whose crosses are heavy and recognizable, and for whom Christ does have a particular compassion.

Yet everyone has some cross to bear: a weakness, a worry, a trouble of some kind.

Thomas à Kempis, the author of *The Imitation of Christ*, shares his insights in a chapter called 'The Royal Way of the Cross' in these words:

> The cross is for ever present and always waits on you. Wherever you run, you cannot escape it. You carry yourself wherever you go. You will always be there. Turn yourself over and under and inside out; you will always find the cross.

Inevitably, overcoming our sins is a life-long challenge. Using the time-honoured weaponry of self-discipline and almsgiving, we make a special effort at this season. However, the battle shouldn't be waged too broadly. Wise guides have suggested that we strive to identify our principal failing, and concentrate on its demise with all our strength.

In the matter of almsgiving, there is no lack of worthy charities; some in dire need. Giving to them should not be regarded guiltily as 'conscience-money', if its aim is the betterment of the human condition or, deeper still, love of our neighbour. Remember the value of even a cup of water given in Christ's name. So we'll decide now which charity to support, and post off our cheque at the start of Lent as an earnest of our sincerity.

When it comes to self-denial, there's no need for gloom. 'Penance' is to be employed as an instrument, not an end in itself. A sensible measure of it should help to achieve something of that humble, contrite heart so praised in Scripture. Let common sense prevail. How rightly we were told as youngsters: 'By all means give up sweets for Lent but, if doing so makes you sulky, get back to your chocolates double-quick.'

Robert Herrick ends his poem about the season with this prescription:

> To show a heart grief-rent,
> To starve thy sin,
> Not bin;
> And that's to keep thy Lent.

The Widow's Mite

I lent my copy of the *Oxford Book of Christian Verse* to someone years ago. Published first in 1940 and edited by Lord David Cecil, it has been out of print for a long time. What a joy it was to have a copy hunted down by a friend recently, and to enjoy afresh many favourite pieces of verse.

One of the shortest poems is based upon this incident recorded in chapter 21 of St Luke's Gospel:

Looking up, Jesus saw rich people putting their offerings into the treasury; and he noticed a poverty-stricken widow putting in two small coins, and he said, 'I tell you truly, this poor widow has put in more than any of them; for these have all put in money they could spare, but she in her poverty has put in all she had to live on.'

The anonymous poem runs as follows:

Two mites, two drops (yet all her house and land),
Falls from a steady heart, though trembling hand:
The other's wanton wealth foams high, and brave,
The other cast away, she only gave.

The 'mites' were copper coins, the smallest in circulation. Jesus praises the generosity of the widow, and the incident prepares the reader to be aware of the generosity of the Lord, the self-effacing, self-giving servant of the Passion narrative.

Moreover, we who endeavour to imitate the perfect example of Jesus should neither shirk nor wish to shirk loving duties of charity when they arise. The ancient treatise of Thomas à Kempis, *The Imitation of Christ*, affirms this:

> Whatever is done out of charity, be it ever so small or insignificant, becomes fully fruitful. For God measures not so much the deed as how great is the motivation for the deed.

Christ's generosity is evident throughout the Gospels, but it is towards the end of his ministry that it shines most gloriously.

Three mighty episodes manifest his love and self-denial quite overwhelmingly. First, the washing of the disciples' feet, where he effectually undertakes the office of a slave to teach us the beauty of humility and the obligation to love one another for his sake; second, the mysterious and moving institution of the Eucharist at the Last Supper, an act of sublime self-giving; and third, the ultimate sacrifice, the crucifixion on Calvary, where he shed his blood and yielded up his spirit for the salvation of the whole world.

There is always room for self-examination in this matter. Our society is so dangerously apt to be selfish and greedy, and none of us is immune from the infection. Millions are in states of direst need, and our baser instincts tell us not to get involved, to pass by on the other side.

The parable of the Good Samaritan was in answer to the lawyer's question: 'Who is my neighbour?' The story over, the Lord tells the man, as he still tells you and me: 'Go and do likewise.' Are we prepared to go, and, having gone, to give?

A Time for Silence

Longfellow's poetry has been out of fashion for many years. A nineteenth-century Harvard academic, widely travelled, he found fame in the US for his verses and in this country was second in popularity only to Tennyson. In my schooldays, his principal champion was our Latin master, who borrowed his words to stimulate his sometimes recalcitrant pupils. 'Life is real, life is earnest' (from *A Psalm of Life*) was a predictable rallying cry upon the near approach of examinations. Nowadays, only a few folk will recall that Longfellow created once much-read works such as *Excelsior* and *The Song of Hiawatha*.

One of the pleasures of poetry is the discovery of lovely surprises, of which I came across an example recently – by H. W. Longfellow. It occurs within a privately circulated anthology. It is a sonnet entitled *Divina Commedia*. Our poet had translated Dante's mighty epic in 1867, and several shorter pieces are indebted to its inspiration. This one tells simply how the poet noticed a labourer coming up quietly to a cathedral door, laying down his burden, entering and kneeling on the floor to pray.

> Far off the noises of the world retreat;
> The loud vociferations of the street
> Became an undistinguishable roar.

The observer is moved to imitate this practice, and to discover that:

> ... the tumult of the time disconsolate
> To inarticulate murmurs dies away,
> While the eternal ages watch and wait.

Certain biblical references accord with those lines, the Pharisee and the publican parable, for instance, or words from Ecclesiastes, chapter 3: 'a time for silence and a time for speech'.

The comforts flowing from the silence may be best articulated by poets, but are experienced by countless others. Who has not yearned to get away from 'the loud vociferations of the street' and even from the 'inarticulate murmurs' granted by closed doors and windows? Yet escape is hard in our workaday world, for few are called to embrace a life dedicated to contemplation, fewer still to that of a hermit.

However, it matters to many to make within their day a regular time, however short, when they can put themselves privately in the presence of God, and pray without interruption in silent reflection. Where such a way is habitual, it may become a source of spiritual reassurance, in the face of any day's testing experiences.

Spoken prayers and public worship are of high value, but peace of soul is often felt to accompany the early morning, before our poet's 'tumult of the time disconsolate' ensues.

> Lord, teach me to silence my own heart, that I may listen to the gentle movement of the Holy Spirit within me, and sense the depths which are of God. (Frankfurt prayer, 16th century)

Peace

The poet Gerard Manley Hopkins asked:

> When will you ever, Peace, wild wooddove, shy wings
> shut,
> Your roaming round me end, and under be my boughs?

It's a cry from the heart from someone whose life was subject to much worry and depression. That peace should keep on roaming round him, without settling, is consonant with his personality. Yet we can all identify with his feelings, for private peace of mind, let alone global peace, is as elusive as it is desirable.

To look around our contemporary world without being concerned about peace would be to live in an ivory tower. Iraq, along with a number of African and South American countries, might spring to mind at first, since their regrettably unstable regimes often make the headlines.

War, and rumours of war, and the consequences of past wars, all of these are a widespread feature of our times. Mark also how peace is missing from units far smaller than nations. Within areas of our own land and its institutions there are elements of disturbance from time to time.

Nor need we focus only upon major cities and their ongoing problems of racism and unemployment. The tiniest rural community might not be immune from wrangling and hostility.

Moreover, misunderstandings and resentments can ruin the harmony of families, where initial antipathies can develop over time into irreconcilable bitterness. Have you never seen sad evidence of this at weddings or even funerals, where relatives must be separated diplomatically so as to avoid a major scene?

And we are shocked, imagining it could never happen to us, but it could.

It's less likely to, however, if we can promote and achieve peace of soul within ourselves. One way to pursue it is to make sure we put aside, daily, some little time for reflection and prayer. This can be done best in solitude, and should become a faithful habit.

A precious period must be found regularly for speaking to God and listening to him. Our Lord's perfect example of personal prayer will serve as our chief inspiration.

Holy men and women down the centuries have pointed us that way. A few dedicated minutes each day will suffice for busy people, but longer if personal lifestyles will allow.

The solitude sought for needn't be found (or be possible) within a chapel or prayer-room. One's car might suit, or a bus or train, or a solitary walk, always providing there isn't too much external noise or any human interruption. It's like a brief sojourn on a hilltop where the view is clearer and the air purer, and we can come down, as it were, from our high point with a calm spirit.

Gerard Manley Hopkins was deeply spiritual, and his troubled soul would be soothed through his peaceful communing with God. Whatever our temperament, the peace of Christ can be ours, too. Take our poet's lovely thought:

> And when Peace here does house
> He comes with work to do,
> he does not come to coo
> He comes to brood and sit.

Bibliography

Albert, E., *History of English Literature* (Harrap, London, 1979).

Allot, K., *The Complete Poems of M. Arnold* (Longman, London, 1965).

Anderson, C. C., *Christian Eloquence: Contemporary Doctrinal Preaching* (Hillenbrand Books, Chicago, 2005).

Anderson, R. S., *The Soul of God: A Theological Memoir* (Wipf and Stock, Eugene, 2004).

Atwan, R. & Wieder, L. (eds.), *Chapters Into Verse: A Selection of Poetry in English Inspired by the Bible from Genesis Through Revelation* (Oxford University Press, Oxford, 2000).

Auden, W. H., *Academic Graffiti* (Faber and Faber, London, 1971).

Bachelor, M. (ed.), *Christian Poetry Collection* (Lion Book, Oxford, 1995).

Battenhouse, R. W. (ed.), *Shakespeare's Christian Dimension: An Anthology of Commentary* (Indiana University Press, Indiana, 1994).

Belloc, H., *On Everything* (Methuen, London, 1910).

Belloc, H., *Sonnets and Verse* (Duckworth, London, 1954).

Benedict XVI, *Jesus of Nazareth*, trans. A. Walker (Bloomsbury, London, 2007).

Bond, H. K., Kunin, S. D. & Murphy, F. A. (eds.), *A Companion to Religious Studies and Theology*, (Edinburgh University Press, Edinburgh, 2003).

Bottrall, R. & M. (ed.), *Collected English Verse* (Sidgewick & Jackson, London, 1947).

Boyle, N., *Sacred and Secular Scriptures: A Catholic Approach to Literature* (Darton, Longman and Todd, London, 2004).

Bradley, Ian (ed.), *The Penguin Book of Hymns* (Penguin Books Ltd., 1990).

Bridges, R., *The Spirit of Man: An Anthology in English & French from the Philosophers & Poets, Made by the Poet Laureate in 1915 & Dedicated by Gracious Permission to His Majesty the King* (Longmans, Green and Co., London, 1923).

Brilioth, Y., *Landmarks in the History of Preaching* (SPCK, London, 1950).

Brown, G. M., *The Year of the Whale* (John Murray, London, 1965).

Burghardt, W. J., *Preaching: The Art and the Craft* (Paulist Press, New York, 1987).

Cameron, J., *The Artist's Way: A Spiritual Path to Higher Creativity* (Souvenir Press, London, 1994).

Charteris, E., *The Life and Letters of Edmund Gosse* (Heinemenn, 1931).

Coote, S., *John Keats: A Life* (Hodder and Stoughton, London, 1995).

Cummings, E. E., *Complete Poems*, Vol. II (Granada, London, 1962).

De Sales, F., *Introduction to the Devout Life* (Everyman, London 1955).

Dickens, C., *Martin Chuzzlewit*, (Nelson Classics, Edinburgh 1964).

Dickinson, E., *The Complete Poems*, ed. T. H. Johnson (Faber & Faber, London, 1975).

Dixon, W. M. & Grierson, H. J. C. (eds.), *The English Parnassus: An Anthology Chiefly of Longer Poems* (Clarendon Press, Oxford, 1921).

Donne, J., *Complete Poetry and Selected Prose*, ed. J. Hayward (Nonesuch Press, 1942).

Drane, J. W., *The McDonaldization of the Church:*

Spirituality, Creativity, and the Future of the Church (Darton, Longman and Todd, London, 2000).

Duffy, E., *Walking to Emmaus* (Burns & Oates, London, 2006).

Feldman, P. R. & Robinson, D. (eds.), *A Century of Sonnets: The Romantic-era Revival, 1750–1850* (Oxford University Press US, 1999).

Fergusson, M., *George Mackay Brown: The Life* (John Murray, London, 2006).

Flannery, A. (ed.), *Vatican Council II: Conciliar and Postconciliar Documents*, (Dominican Publications, Dublin, 1992).

Foley, E., *Preaching Basics: A Model and a Method* (Archdiocese of Chicago, Liturgy Training Publications, Chicago, 1998).

Glazier. M. & Hellwig, M. (eds.), *The Modern Catholic Encyclopaedia* (Gill and Macmillan, Dublin, 1994).

Gledhill, R. (ed.), *The Times Book of Best Sermons* (Cassell, London, 1998).

Goudge, E., *A Book of Comfort* (Collins, Glasgow, 1982).

Graves, R., *Collected Poems* (Guild Publishing, London, 1975).

Heaney, S., *The Redress of Poetry: Oxford Lectures* (Faber & Faber, London, 1995).

Heille, G., *Theology of Preaching: Essays on Vision and Mission in the Pulpit* (Melisande, London, 2001).

Hendrie, R., *Go, Tell Them: Thoughts Towards a Theology of Preaching* (St Paul's, London, 2006).

Herbert, G., *The Country Parson*, ed. R. Blythe (Canterbury Press, Norwich, 2003).

Higham, F., *Lancelot Andrewes* (SCM Press, London, 1952).

Hill, G., *Collected Poems* (Andre Deutsch, London, 1978).

Hopkins, G. M., *Poems,* ed. W. H. Gardner (Oxford University Press, London, 1964).

Houselander, C., *The Stations of the Cross* (Hart Books, London, 1955).

Hughes, T., *Remains of Elmet* (Faber and Faber, London, 1979).

Janowiak, P., *The Holy Preaching: The Sacramentality of the Word in the Liturgical Assembly* (Liturgical Press, Collegeville, Minnesota, 2000).

Johnston, G., *Preaching to a Postmodern World: A Guide to Reaching Twenty-first-century Listeners* (Intervarsity Press, Nottingham, 2001).

Kavanagh, A., *On Liturgical Theory* (The Liturgical Press, Collegeville, Minnesota, 1984).

Kenner, C. S., 'Matthew 28:16-20', in *The Lectionary Commentary: Theological Exegesis for Sunday's Texts*, ed. R. E. Van Harn (Erdman's Publishing Co., Grand Rapids, Michigan, 2001).

Kleiser, G., *How to Argue and Win* (Funk and Wagnells Co., New York, 1912).

Knight, W. A. (ed.), *Colloquia Peripatetica: Notes of Conversations with J. Duncan* (David Douglas, Edinburgh, 1879).

Knox, R. A., *Pastoral Sermons* (Burns Oates, London, 1959).

Knox, R. A., *A Retreat for Priests* (Sheed & Ward, London, 1946).

Lamb, C., *Prose and Poetry* (Clarendon, Oxford, 1924).

Lash, N., *Holiness, Speech and Silence: Reflections on the Question of God* (Ashgate, London, 2004).

Leeson, E. (ed.), *The MacMillan Anthology of English Prose* (Papermac, London, 1994).

Lefebvre, P. & Mason, C. (eds.), *John Henry Newman in his Time* (Family Publications, Oxford, 2007).

Lewis, C. S., *Letters to Malcolm* (Geoffrey Bles, London, 1963).

Lowry, E. L., *The Homiletical Plot: The Sermon as Narrative Art Form* (Westminster/John Knox Press, London, 2001).

Lynd, R., *The Art of Letters* (Duckworth, London, 1928).

MacCaig, N., *Collected Poems* (Chatto & Windus, London, 1990).

MacNeice, L., *The Collected Poems*, ed. E. R. Dodds (Faber & Faber, London, 1966).

Macpherson, D., *Homiletics and Lection* (Maryvale Institute, Birmingham, 2005).

Martin, R. B., *Gerard Manley Hopkins: A Very Private Life* (Flamingo, London, 1992).

McCracken, R., *The Making of the Sermon* (SCM Press Ltd., London, 1956).

Monshau, M. (ed.), *The Grace and Task of Preaching* (Dominican Publications, Dublin, 2006).

North, P. N. & North, J. (eds.), *Scared Space: House of God, Gate of Heaven* (Continuum, London, 2007).

O'Collins, G. & Farrugia, M., *Catholicism: The Story of Catholic Christianity* (Oxford University Press, Oxford, 2003).

Oxford Book of Christian Verse, ed. D. Cecil (Clarendon Press, Oxford, 1941).

Oxford Book of English Literature, 5th edition (Oxford University Press, Oxford, 1989).

Oxford Companion to 20th-Century Poetry, ed. I. Hamilton (Clarendon Press, Oxford, 1994).

Palgrave, F. T., *Palgrave's The Golden Treasury* (Oxford University Press, Oxford, 1914).

Pearson, H. (ed.), *The Smith of Smiths* (The Folio Society, London, 1977).

Ramsey, B., *Beginning to Read the Fathers* (Paulist Press, London, 1985).

Radcliffe, T., 'The World Shall Come to Walsingham', in *Sacred Space: House of God, Gate of Heaven*, ed. P. North and J. North (Continuum, London, 2007).

Radcliffe, T., *What is the Point of Being a Christian?* (Burns & Oates, London, 2005).

Schiller, F., *Naïve and Sentimental Poetry*, tr. W. F. Maitland (Blackwell Publishers, 1951).

Schmemann, A., *The World as Sacrament* (Darton, Longman & Todd, London, 1966).

Shakespeare, W., *The Complete Works*, ed. S. W. Wells and G. Taylor (Clarendon Press, Oxford, 1988).

Shaw, G. B., *The Complete Plays of George Bernard Shaw* (Odham's Press Ltd., London, 1934).

Smyth, C. H. E., *The Art of Preaching* (SPCK, London, 1964).

Southey, R., *The Doctor*, Vol. I (Longman, Rees, Orme, Brown, Green and Longman, London, 1834).

The Tablet, issues of 26.5.07 (Radcliffe) and 21.7.07 (O'Leary) (Tablet Publishing Co., London, 2007).

Thomas, R. S., *Collected Poems 1945–1990* (Phoenix Giant, London, 1993).

Trevelyan, G. M., *A Layman's Love of Letters* (Longmans, Green & Co., London, 1954).

Tugwell, S. (ed.), 'Treatise on the formation of preachers, no. 70', in *Early Dominicans: Selected Writings* (Paulist Press, New York, 1982).

US Conference of Bishops, *Fulfilled in Your Hearing*, (Washington, DC, 1982).

Vagaggini, C., *Theological Dimensions of the Liturgy: A General Treatise on the Theology of the Liturgy*, trans. L. J. Doyle and W. A. Jurgens (Liturgical Press, Collegeville, Minnesota, 1976).

Van Doren, M., *One Hundred Poems Selected by the Author* (Hill & Wang, New York, 1967).

Von Hugel, F., *Essays and Addresses on the Philosophy of Religion*, 1st series (J. M. Dent & Sons, London, 1921).

Waterhouse, E. (ed.), *A Little Book of Life and Death* (Methuen, London, 1902).

Wavell, A. P., *Other Men's Flowers: An Anthology of Poetry* (Pimlico, London, 1992).

Wordsworth, W., *Ecclesiastical Sonnets, Complete Works of William Wordsworth* (New York, 1880).

Worlock, D., *Take One at Bedtime* (Sheed & Ward, London, 1962).

Waznak, R. P., *An Introduction to the Homily* (Liturgical Press, Collegeville, Minnesota, 1988).

Lightning Source UK Ltd.
Milton Keynes UK
23 November 2010

163308UK00002B/6/P